'There are no victims in show business. Everybody in show business deserves each other.'

Art Murphy, box-office analyst, *Daily Variety*

Money and Power in the Movies Today

NICOLAS KENT

St. Martin's Press
New York

To
EDWINA AND PETER
and
RODNEY AND JO.

ISBN 0-312-07040-3

First published in Great Britain by BBC Books, a division of BBC Enterprises
Limited.

First U.S. Edition: August 1991
10 9 8 7 6 5 4 3 2 1

CONTENTS

ACKNOWLEDGEMENTS   6

1   CITY OF ANGELS   9

2   CLAY FEET AND THE
    BOTTOM LINE   40

3   HEAVENLY BODIES   78

4   SCHMUCKS WITH APPLES   115

5   HUSTLER-ARTISTS   147

6   FIRE-FIGHTERS AND FORTUNE-
    HUNTERS   178

7   PIGGIES IN THE MIDDLE   210

SOURCE NOTES   245

BIBLIOGRAPHY   250

INDEX   252

PICTURE CREDITS   256

ACKNOWLEDGEMENTS

Given the subject of this book, I think it is appropriate to begin by thanking my agent, Mark Lucas, who has been a constant source of good advice and encouragement. My editors, Heather Holden-Brown and Susan Martineau, displayed infinite patience as they saw one deadline after another pass into history with no sign of my manuscript. Art Director, Frank Phillips, and everyone at BBC Books seemed to be enthusiastic and supportive. Valuable advice was supplied by Sonia Rosario, Carol Rothkopf and Steve and Pat Hanson. Their suggestions were always well-judged and helpful. I am grateful to Alan Yentob and Michael Jackson at the BBC. Without their faith and enthusiasm, none of this would have been possible. Among the team who helped me make the documentary series, *Naked Hollywood*, the contributions by Margy Kinmonth, Alan Lewens, John Whiston, Liz Stevens and Andy Paterson stand out. Margy, Alan and John directed their respective episodes. Margy also doubled as a unit photographer, which even in Hollywood is an unusual hyphenate. Liz displayed enormous reserves of tolerance and worked much too hard. Andy's help in producing the series was indispensable and I am especially grateful to him.

I wrote and researched this book over two years from the beginning of 1989 to October 1990. I have tried to mention everyone whose participation in one form or another allowed me to carry out the job I set out to do. Some made greater contributions than others but in the interests of tact and economy, all names are arranged in strict alphabetical order.

Steve Abbott, Geoff Ammer, Steve Arenas, Alan Barker, Peter Bart, Martin Bauer, Hercules Bellville, Peter Benedek, Mark Bentley, Roger Birnbaum, Sara Black, Paul Bloch, Mel Bourne, Leslie Bradley-Marshall, Howard Brandy, Pat Broeske, Nadia Bronson, Mel Brooks, James L. Brooks, Jerry Bruckheimer, James Caan, Michael Caton-Jones, Ronni Chasen, Stan

Chervin, Joan Churchill, Michael Cieply, Joan Cohen, Sam Cohn, Martin Cooper, Roger Corman, Tim Corrie, Jim Crabbe, Cameron Crowe, Joe Dante, Samantha Dean, Peter Dekom, Jonathan Derby, Barry Diller, Lindsay Doran, Mario Dubois, John Gregory Dunne, Nora Ephron, Julius Epstein, Freddie Fields, Paul Flaherty, Charles Flemming, Joey Forsyte, Jodie Foster, Roger Friedman, Graham Fuller, Lowell Ganz, Terry Gilliam, Lawrence Gordon, Brian Grazer, Mike Gruskoff, Sabrina Guinness, Tim Harris, Roz Heller, Manny Hernandez, Scott Herring, Debra Hill, Mike Hoffman, Peter Hoffman, Andrea Jaffe, Dennis Jones, Loretha Jones, Michael Josephson, Karen Kaplan, Elizabeth Kaye, George Kirgo, Bonni Lee, James Lee, Richard LeGravenese, Gerry Lewis, Jane Lewis, Sandy Lieberson, Ed Limato, Jeffrey Logsdon, Kurt Luedtke, Jay Maloney, Babaloo Mandel, Robert Marich, Tony Mark, Penny Marshall, Kim Masters, Rick McCallum, Guy McElwaine, Thomas McCormack, David McJunkin, Mike Medavoy, Joe Medjuck, Katherine Moore, Robert Mundy, Art Murphy, Karen Murphy, Lynda Obst, Charlotte Parker, Dennis Petroskey, Julia Philips, Susan Pile, Louis Pitt, Sydney Pollack, Jeremy Pollard, Tom Pollock, Stephanie Pond Smith, John Powers, Frank Price, Steve Randall, Jane Rees, Ivan Reitman, Maggie Renzi, Elaina Richardson, Phil Alden Robinson, Judith Robson, Howard Rodman, Deborah Rosen, Michael Rosenberg, Joe Roth, Ed Russell, Mark Rydell, Murray Salem, Joy Sapieka, John Sayles, Mary Schulman, Tom Schulman, Arnold Schwarzenegger, Martin Scorsese, Tony Scott, Tom Sherak, Roger Simon, Don Simpson, Sally Van Slyke, Bette Smith, Hy Smith, Steven Soderbergh, David Spady, Dawn Steel, Ueli Steiger, Bill and Fritz Steinkamp, Rick Stevenson, Oliver Stone, Ned Tanen, Sarah Teale, Anne Thompson, Robert Towne, Robert Townsend, Art Vitarella, Harold Vogel, Bruce Wagner, Rupert Walters, Neville Watchurst, Sigourney Weaver, Nick Wechsler, Herschel Weingrod, Bob and Harvey Weinstein, Paula Weinstein, Eric Weissmann, Jay Weston, Jim Wiatt, Michael Williams Jones, Carey Woods, Richard and Lili Fini Zanuck, Jeremy Zimmer.

CHAPTER ONE

CITY OF ANGELS

Strip the phony tinsel off Hollywood and you'll find the real tinsel underneath.

Oscar Levant

I only go to Los Angeles when I am paid for it.

Robert De Niro

Imagine you are flying over Los Angeles. If you look down as your plane banks above the city you will see a giant grid of tiny, neat homes, spotted with swimming-pools, crammed like lemmings to the very edge of the shore. Depending on the wind that day, Los Angeles may be over-shadowed by a beige stain which spreads for miles out to sea. The smog, as famous a local landmark as Grauman's Chinese Theatre and the Hollywood Bowl, seems to cocoon the city and its inhabitants from the outside world. The sense that life here exists inside a bubble is in no way diminished once your feet have touched the ground.

Touch down. A sudden jolt; engines screaming; 400 guts lurch a little; 800 ears experience a momentary deafness; shudder to a stop, catch your breath and shuffle out of one cocoon and into another. Flying into LAX is no different from arriving at any other international airport. As usual, the commands of the stewardess – *fasten your seat belts, ladies and gentlemen, and please remain in your seats until the plane has come to a complete stop* – are spoken in the soothing tone of

An angel's eye view of the city.

a weary mother. There is nothing strange about that in itself. It's just that being treated like a child seems appropriate when you are about to arrive in Los Angeles. Welcome to Hollywood. A place where growing up is optional because dreams can come true.

Fifteen minutes after the jet's wheels have hit the tarmac, 400 bemused passengers, newly released from captivity, blink in the sunlight. Like dream-drugged moviegoers they step outside and, for a moment, they are utterly lost. They have forgotten that this other world ever existed. This trance-like state is common to airline passengers. But normally it evaporates. Here in Los Angeles, inside the bubble, the trance persists. This is not from any sense of dislocation. Quite the opposite because, even if this is your first trip to LA, it all seems so familiar. The light (so bright), the sky (brilliant blue), the ocean (ditto), the beaches (golden), the blondes (beautiful), the automobiles (convertible, stretched, spotless), the palms, the surfers . . . all the bit players we know so well from a hundred movies, a thousand TV shows.

The strongest jolt of *déjà vu* hits you almost immediately. Moments

Driving on the Los Angeles freeways is a dreamlike experience.

after collecting your luggage and your rental car you're gliding down the 405 (San Diego) freeway. Of all that is cinematic to Los Angeles, this is the ultimate. Los Angeles is freeway city. Twenty-six of them girdle LA, covering some 700 miles between Ventura, San Bernardino and Laguna. Framed within the windscreen, the freeways are pure cinema, in 70 mm and sensoround. 'Running with the freeways at night encourages dreaming,' recalls journalist Tom Huth. 'The freeways are so smooth that one can lose all sense of motion, the curves so graceful that the steering wheel seems to move of its own accord ... The people who created our freeways certainly never intended them to be driven by motorists using only 10 per cent of their brain cells, with the other 90 per cent off in space. But this is the result of such peerless design – raceways stripped of all activity but the performance of non-stop driving, whole hillsides blasted away to ensure uneventful passage – a total autopian environment in which monotony leads ineluctably to hallucination.' The freeways are seductive and inspiring. The idea for the movie, *Absence of Malice*, came to screenwriter, Kurt Luedtke, on the freeway. His dreams came true but how many millions more have been still-born at 70 mph?

Leaving LAX and the screaming jets behind, you head north on the 405 to Sunset. By now the sense of cinematic *déjà vu* is so potent that you are feeling like the lead player in your own biopic. Take a left on Sunset, past the manicured lawns of Bel-Air and Beverly Hills. A perfect backdrop. Roll credits. Hollywood is only moments away. Savour the anticipation. What do you expect? Like most people – the millions who know only the flickering images – you will have a notion of Hollywood, an idea that might seem even more vivid than the memory of your own home town. It is the Mecca of Show Business. It is the Promised Land. It is Glamour City. It is Sodom-by-the-Sea. It is fame, wealth, sex, power. It is the perfect manifestation of the American Dream.

Driving down Sunset, you pass by the Beverly Hills Hotel, a popular venue for breakfast meetings between film folk.

Keep east on Sunset and see for yourself. The reality is a disappointment. Hollywood today is a dormitory suburb, and the boulevard that bisects it is made up of images from a handful of tatty postcards – a star-studded sidewalk, an ancient steak house, an elaborate Chinese movie palace, a gaudy shopping strip for trippers. Is this really Hollywood? Yes and no. No, because Hollywood is far more than the shanty town remains of Grauman's Chinese Theatre, Musso and Franks, and the star-spangled sidewalk. Hollywood is the movie business, and today the business of making movies is about as big as any business gets. The dingy stores on Hollywood Boulevard give the impression that the movie colony is virtually extinct but the truth is quite the reverse. Movies are in demand. The arrival of the video-cassette has spawned a generation who are eager to gorge themselves on movies at home. New television channels are being launched across Europe and after the fall of the Iron Curtain it is only a matter of time before capitalism's insatiable appetite for entertainment spreads east. And from where does the vast majority of this entertainment originate? Today, at least for some, Hollywood is a boom town at the height of its prosperity.

But in other ways, the shanty town aura of Hollywood Boulevard is much closer to the movie business and Los Angeles than its inhabitants would like to admit. Hollywood Boulevard is like the discarded skin, the carapace, shed by a pragmatic and wily beast that has struggled from its cocoon to assume some other form, but with only partial success. Despite the big league prosperity of the modern movie business – second only to the defence industry as America's largest export earner – and despite the city's efforts to turn itself into a cosmopolitan metropolis, neither the business nor Los Angeles can entirely rid themselves of Hollywood Boulevard and all that it signifies. Their failure to disassociate themselves from the past is certainly not for lack of trying. Angelenos never tire of explaining

Old Hollywood's big names are immortalized in cement on Hollywood Boulevard.

that there is far more to Los Angeles than Hollywood and the movies. 'To think of Los Angeles as Hollywood-driven is to think of London as Princess Di-driven,' says one exasperated native. But to the outside world, and to many people who live here, LA,

Hollywood and the movies are one and the same. To those resentful locals who have and want no part of the movie business it must seem sometimes as if Los Angeles has been hijacked by a tawdry suburb that occupies only a fraction of its area. But Hollywood Boulevard is a stubborn reminder of where the movie business and the city came from. It is a part of its past and its present.

All cities carry with them the scent of their beginnings and the odour of Hollywood evokes that of the gold rush. That scent is still strong and it is given visible form by Hollywood Boulevard. Budd Schulberg probably put it best. Schulberg was born with a celluloid spoon in his mouth – he was the son of a Hollywood mogul. In his classic novel of rampant ambition, *What Makes Sammy Run?*, he observed the internal rhythms of the movie colony during its so-called golden age, the thirties and forties, with a native's insight. 'The gold rush was probably the only other set-up where so many people could hit the jackpot and the skids this close together.' According to Schulberg, Hollywood had become 'a major industry without losing the crazy fever of a gold-boom town'. His memorable protagonist, the insatiable Sammy Glick, was a prototype for every hustler on the make who has headed west since then. Some things do not change. Fifty years later the city still exudes the sweet stench of gold-rush fever. 'Los Angeles has never been viewed as a city but as a place where hustlers come,' says Robert Towne, a native Angeleno and the Oscar-winning screenwriter of *Chinatown*, the most vivid portrayal of LA on screen. 'It's like a movie and everyone's trying to hit the main vein.'

'It's like a movie,' says Towne. What more concise explanation could there be for the waves of pilgrims who continue to make the long trek west? Even the tales of corruption and tragedy have been romanticized and woven into the myth. Even the odds against success, the million routine failures add to the city's lustre. It's like a movie. The very fact that Los Angeles appears to be exactly as you

Chinatown, written by a native Angeleno, Robert Towne, is a story of corruption and greed acted out against a backdrop of dazzling sunlight and inky shadows.

might have imagined it should put you on your guard. That first wave of *déjà vu* out on the freeway is dangerously deceptive. It encourages you to believe that dreams can come true. It tempts you to participate in the illusion. Anything seems possible. All you need is one lucky break. And that desperate, intoxicating hope is not yours alone. It has been shared, is shared, by countless thousands of like-minded hopefuls. How else can you explain why so many come here to fulfil some cherished dream and then stay long after their fledgling hopes have been so completely snuffed out? The Hollywood dreamers wait at tables, valet park limousines, obediently serve the members of a club they would kill to join. All they need is one lucky break. It's just a matter of chance. And who can say they are wrong? The right break at the right time has worked for so many others.

There are no rules in Hollywood, as Kurt Luedtke found out when he abandoned a successful career in journalism – he was editor of *The Detroit Free Press* – so that he could try his hand at writing screenplays. His subsequent experience was straight out of a Hollywood fairy tale. His first script, *Absence of Malice*, was made into a movie starring Paul Newman and Sally Field, and directed by Sydney Pollack. His second screenwriting effort was *Out of Africa*, for which he won an Oscar. Luedtke readily admits to his good fortune. 'It's an incredibly complicated, very capricious business in which nobody really knows what's going to work and what isn't going to work,' he says. 'Making even a half-decent movie requires, apart from a lot of money and a lot of talent, no small degree of plain luck. Every time somebody asserts a rule about any part of movie-making, I tend to think that it's a rule that's made to be broken. The critical thing is that nobody knows what's going to work until you do it.'

The many who have not and will never make it in Hollywood console themselves with the knowledge that success is a matter of luck, and luck can smile on anyone any time. According to the anthropologist Hortense Powdermaker it was just the same with their ancestors. 'It is far easier in Hollywood than elsewhere for a person ... to believe that his lack of success is due only to not getting the breaks,' she wrote some forty-five years ago, 'because almost everyone, successful and unsuccessful, talented and mediocre, regards those same breaks as the most important factor in success.'

For those who are still waiting for their lucky break, the fact that the fruits of success are so abundantly on display must help those crushed hopes to linger on. Nowhere else do the wealthy consume so conspicuously as in California. In such an open-air society, material rewards are openly displayed. Wealth, like health, should be seen. Hollywood is a carnival of success and those that fail but stay on are the mute audience, transfixed by the spectacle. Everywhere, the trappings of achievement are available to the eye – see but don't touch – like the parade of prizes that adorn a countless succession of TV game shows.

The homes of the hyper-successful are monuments to their own self-satisfaction. The secluded environs of Beverly Hills and Bel-Air are routinely disrupted by a renewed bout of construction as a mere mansion is razed to the ground to make way for the latest replica of a European palace, exact in every detail, only bigger. Aaron Spelling, the producer of *Dynasty*, tore down Bing Crosby's old house in Holmby Hills to make way for a 56 500 square foot mega-mansion. Alexander Coler, a local property developer who has erected his fair share of modern palaces for the super-rich, recently built himself a new home in Beverly Hills. 'The architect who designed this house thought this would be a nice crowning point to my career,' he told the *Los Angeles Times*. The new house features an indoor swimming-pool, a disco, a library, two gyms, a two-lane bowling alley, servants' apartments and a museum. Mr Coler is building himself a second home in Palm Springs, this one with its own golf course.

If it is truly more difficult for a rich man to enter the kingdom of Heaven than it is for a camel to pass through the eye of a needle, then Hollywood must be Hell's waiting-room on earth. The riches accumulated by some of Hollywood's highest earners dwarf the gross national products of several of the world's smaller nations. Here, as estimated by *Forbes* magazine, are the 1989 gross incomes of a clutch of top entertainers: Mel Gibson, actor, $11 million (following *Lethal Weapon*, his price soared to $10 million per movie); Bill Murray, actor, $17 million; Jack Nicholson, actor, $34 million; Arnold Schwarzenegger, actor, $35 million; Sylvester Stallone, actor,

$38 million (*Forbes* reported Stallone received an upfront payment of $25 million for *Rocky V*); Steven Spielberg, director, $64 million. We're talking serious money here.

'It's a society of conspicuous consumption in which money is extremely overvalued,' says Sam Cohn, a New York-based talent agent who represents some of the biggest names in the movies and on stage. Despite his prominence in the entertainment business he spends as little time as possible in Los Angeles. 'I would describe it as a societal disease. I mean, there are many artists and there are many executives, whom we all know, who personally have fortunes that far exceed any need they may have for the rest of their lives. But in a cultural way that becomes a personal validation. It's a substitute for achievement.' In a strange way, these enormous fees seem to make everyone feel better, not just the recipient but also the donor. Studio executives who gamble these millions on a hunch can delude themselves that the size of their investment gives credence to their instincts and belies the fact that making movies is, was, and always will be, a crap shoot. And, of course, inflated prices for star talent translates eventually into rising salaries and bumper bonuses for the executives themselves.

'Money and power are interchangeable commodities in this business,' says writer-director Paul Schrader. Schrader was raised a Calvinist and might, under different circumstances, have become a minister. Instead he went on to write a slew of highly regarded screenplays, including *Taxi Driver*, before moving on to direct the scripts he wrote. 'I think of money as an extension of power. I love to get huge salaries, not because I need the money, or want to own a lot of shit. But I love to make money because that's power . . . And the more money you make, the more power you have. People are going to respect a writer they pay $250 000 for a script more than a writer they pay $50 000. They are going to take your opinion a lot more seriously if they pay you more money, because they can't think

KROCH'S & BRENTANO'S
835 N. MICHIGAN AVE.
WATER TOWER PLAZA

SALE   001705 0017 004 00004 06298
          12/28/93   04:24 PM

GDSEN 0
SALE BOOKS 1 @   4.97
  TKT 9.95 50% OFF
SALE BOOKS 1 @   11.97
  TKT 23.95 50% OFF
          SUB TOTAL   16.94
     8.750%   TAX   1.48
             TOTAL   18.42
            AMEX   18.42
AUTH: 000036
WING/LA
1295 373217909782004

ALL REFUNDS REQUIRE RECEIPTS

of themselves as having made a mistake.'

Money matters in Hollywood. In such an insecure society where success or failure can occur quite by accident, there is a superstitious belief that by making your achievements visible, tangible, they thus become permanent. And, as Schrader points out, money denotes muscle. It is a symbol of that most potent of Hollywood buzz words, 'leverage'. In the *Shorter Oxford English Dictionary*, leverage is defined as 'the mechanical advantage gained by the use of a lever'. In the lexicon of Hollywood, leverage 'denotes the ability to control a person or situation to your own advantage'. Leverage is an abstract concept but it is easily recognizable. People with leverage have 'heat' – another buzz word. They get the best tables in restaurants; they have court-side season tickets to the Lakers basketball games; their services are desired by every producer and studio in town; they have gross points in the movies they make; they're hot. But leverage really comes into its own when movie people engage in Hollywood's most popular indoor sport – making deals. Dealmaking is to movie people what the tea ceremony is to the Japanese. They are very, very serious about it. When people with leverage make a deal, they always walk away with more money than they did the last time, and that is a very great deal of money indeed.

'Money is a tool of power, a way of being seen, a way of showing you're successful, of being one of the rich and famous,' says Michael Josephson. Josephson was a successful publisher of legal textbooks before he opted to found the non-profit-making Institute for the Advancement of Ethics in memory of his parents. Since then, the Institute has advised many commercial and political groups on ways to foster ethical working practices. Sitting in his office in Marina del Rey, observed by a bronze bust of Abraham Lincoln, his personal hero, he speaks about Hollywood with the detachment of an interested observer. Josephson thinks of Hollywood as divided into two basic classes. 'There is the underclass who are just struggling to get a job, to be an extra,' he says, 'and they would literally do it for free just to get the exposure. And then you have the successful class who compete only among each other in which case they have to have a way of rating themselves. The truth of the matter is, once you make a certain amount of money, the increments don't make a difference to your lifestyle. They have to be driven by something else. It's the acknowledgment, the success, the winning.'

The desire to succeed is by no means peculiar to Hollywood but here it is pronounced to an excessive extent. Working in the movies is lucrative and all-absorbing. In Hollywood it is common for people to admit that they literally live their work. Hollywood insiders take their rigorous work ethic for granted but to those who come from outside the community, the pitch at which people pace themselves is striking. Ed Limato is a good case in point. He is one of the town's most powerful talent agents, representing such stars as Mel Gibson, Richard Gere, Michelle Pfeiffer and Matthew Modine amongst others. 'In Hollywood, I think you really have to eat it, breathe it every waking moment of the day,' he says. 'It's an eighteen-hour job. You're in the office early. You're on the telephones all day. If you have a lunch, it's a business lunch. It's either with a producer, a studio head, a client. I usually work until eight in the evening. I never leave here before eight in the evening and then I go directly to dinner, again with a client or a producer or a studio head. Then I go home, and I have to read a script and either I read half of it or all of it, and then I pick it up the next morning and start all over again.'

Given the exaggerated degree to which people live their work, it naturally follows that their own sense of identity is tightly bound up with their professional success. Winning matters, more profoundly in Hollywood than anywhere else it seems. In a city which has the mentality of a gold-boom town, where so many live their work, people define themselves by their success. Pick up a copy of *Daily Variety*, commonly known as the bible of the entertainment industry, and you will find pages of advertisements trumpeting the latest breaks: the weekend grosses of such and such a movie; the signing of so-and-so to appear in Mr Producer's forthcoming blockbuster; the completion of principal photography on the greatest movie ever made. It's not just a case of, 'If you've got it, flaunt it!' Each advertisement is like a talisman. It wards off what everyone fears most in Hollywood, failure.

This is not a town for losers. As Michael Josephson says, 'It is not only winning that is very important for Hollywood. It's not losing. There's a real concern in Hollywood about losing or being identified with losing and having your winning streak broken. The fact of the matter is that when you do lose, you have a bad movie, people step back from you a little bit.' This tendency to cling to people with unbroken records deters the taking of risks and means that Hollywood is not always as creative as it ought to be. According to Terry Gilliam, director of *Time Bandits*, *Brazil* and *The Adventures of Baron Munchausen*, 'The problem here is that people want success so desperately. It's how they keep their jobs. So the best thing is to play safe. When you start taking chances, you're going out on a limb. It might pay off; it may not pay off. But a lot of people who have risen are people who play safe.'

In Hollywood people are haunted by the anonymity of failure. To fail is to become instantly invisible. 'People get a smell about a movie before it opens,' says ex-studio boss Ned Tanen. 'It's amazing how no one talks about it.' No one returns your calls; your regular corner table at Morton's, just by the bar, isn't as frequently available as it used to be; at parties, the few you still attend, you find yourself reduced to talking about the weather; life stops being fun. It was just the same back in the forties. 'A man out of a job is usually a man out of friends,' wrote Hortense Powdermaker. 'There seems to be a belief that success or failure is contagious through contact, a sort of sympathetic magic.'

Ex-studio boss Ned Tanen has survived at the top longer than most movie executives even though he has known his fair share of failure.

However, although the pitch of competition in Hollywood is ferocious, it is evident that movie people also need each other. At Le Dome, the town's premier 'power restaurant', the who's who of Hollywood disconnect themselves from their telephones for a couple of hours to press flesh and make deals. Walk in there at lunch time, if you can get a table, and feel the heat. The intensity of the competition in that room makes the air quiver. But there's something else there too, a desperate dependency. Hollywood people need each other, not all the time, but at least for today. According to Ned Tanen, 'It's a kind of love-hate family relationship where they are not necessarily wishing their best friends well, but they cling to each other in some form of desperation.'

Forty-five years ago Hortense Powdermaker observed the same phenomenon. 'There is a constant jockeying for superior position and power but while the competition is hard and severe, there is among the competitors a great need for each other. The overt verbal behaviour in all these relationships is that of love and friendship. Warm words of endearment and great cordiality set the tone. But underneath is hostility amounting frequently to hatred, and, even more important, a lack of respect for each other's work. To the casual observer all relations seem to be on a remarkably personal level. But this is merely a sugar-coating for a deep impersonality. This impersonality comes out in two important ways. People are property in no uncertain terms, usually valuable property, and everyone has his price. Underlying the endearing terms of every conversation are the questions: "What can I get from him?" ... "What does he want from me?" ... "Will I need him in the future, if not now?" Human relationships are regarded as basically manipulative and are lacking in all dignity.'

Today the lavish endearments are still a staple of social intercourse in Hollywood but under certain circumstances the underlying tensions and the frenzied urge to succeed are perhaps more readily apparent. Recently, the dramatist and screenwriter, David Mamet, has echoed and updated Powdermaker's comments on the way in which this notion of people as property manifests itself. 'We permit ourselves to be treated like commodities in the hope that we may, one day, be treated like *valuable* commodities,' he says. According to Mamet, who satirized the town with a surgeon's skill in his play, *Speed the Plow*, 'the callousness which passes for Refreshing Frankness in many Hollywood dealings doesn't exist as a direct way to expedite a difficult business – it exists ... because we view each other as bargaining chips, and we tend to think thus: "I can treat you any way I like, because, *if you need something from me*, you have no recourse, and I'm letting you know it."' Michael Josephson thinks that among agents, studio executives and producers there is a growing tendency to spice their language with metaphors of war and gamesmanship. The ferocity of the competition is becoming visible in the words people use. The most notorious example of this kind of verbal brutality, notorious because it actually became public, is the case of Michael Ovitz and Joe Eszterhas.

Michael Ovitz is the chief of Creative Artists Agency, Hollywood's hottest talent agency. He is widely reputed to be the most powerful man in the movie business. Joe Eszterhas is a successful screenwriter and his agent was Michael Ovitz. Towards the end of 1989, Eszterhas met Ovitz and told him he wanted to switch to another agency. Following their meeting, on 3 October Eszterhas sent Ovitz a letter which has since entered Hollywood lore. According to Eszterhas, Ovitz made some rather elaborate threats at their meeting. 'You told me that if I left – "my foot soldiers who go up and down Wilshire Boulevard each day will blow your brains out,"' alleged Eszterhas. Ovitz denied that events had unfolded in the way Eszterhas described them but that didn't stop the satirical magazine, *Spy*, publishing the Ovitz-Eszterhas letters in full. For a brief moment the story even made national news. In retrospect no one really believes that Michael Ovitz meant to kill Joe Eszterhas, but the language is noteworthy. In Hollywood today, metaphors of war are in vogue.

'Killing the opponent, stomping, wiping them out. The language constantly shows this kind of competitiveness, which incidentally also dehumanizes your opponents in some way,' says Michael Josephson. 'When you're in a face-to-face negotiation, that person is no longer someone who's your friend, although they may be. They are the enemy. They are the other side. They are the target. And unfortunately when you use metaphors of war, you often use techniques of war. If this is war, lying is OK, being brutal is OK. I think that pervades a great deal of Hollywood dealmaking.'

One reason why movie people are prone to play war games may be because it is so difficult to draw a line between fact and fiction. Movie people have a licence to create imaginary worlds, to make their dreams come true, and because they are 'artists', it seems they tend to consider themselves immune from the bounds that restrain other people. They live in a world apart, subject to their own laws, their own sense of right and wrong. The callousness with which they behave inside Hollywood contrasts with their unease when they stray outside the community. There is a sense that people who live in Hollywood, which is a world that they have created and can control, are uncomfortable living beyond the confines of that world. Elsewhere is alien territory. They want no part of it. 'California is an isolated state,' says Ned Tanen. 'When you come to California, you either come over an ocean or you come across 1000 miles of desert. It's just here alone. It is, in some ways, Babylon. And it's very easy for people in this business to become very self-involved, not to have a real view of what's going on in the world, and frankly not much interest. Most of the people I've known over the years in this business, really only deal with each other, and they're very comfortable dealing with each other.'

In the forties Hollywood was dubbed 'sunny Siberia'. 'Hollywood people are afraid to leave Hollywood,' was how Gottfried Reinhardt, a producer for Louis B. Mayer, described his neighbours. 'Out in the world, they are frightened. They are unsure of themselves. They never enjoy themselves out of Hollywood.' At around the same time as Reinhardt was grumbling about the timidity of his fellow moviemakers, Hortense Powdermaker wrote that, 'Most of the inhabitants seem to enjoy and receive a certain security from being only with people like themselves. Members of a Melanesian tribe in the South-west Pacific likewise cannot imagine living anywhere else and are fearful of going beyond their own small community.'

Powdermaker had done considerable field work with the islanders in the South-west Pacific and between 1946 and 1947 she decided to apply those same field techniques to the exotic natives of Southern California. The result of her studies, *Hollywood, The Dream Factory*, remains to this day a seminal work. Like all conscientious academics, Powdermaker prefaced her conclusions with a statement of her qualifications as a 'detached scientist'. 'Most important,' she wrote, 'was the absence of any desire on my part to find a job in the movie industry or to become a part of it. This was unique for anyone living in Hollywood for a year.' To Powdermaker, 'the handsome stars with their swimming-pool homes were no more glamorous than were the South Sea aborigines exotic. All, whether ex-cannibal chiefs, magicians, front-office executives, or directors, were human beings working and living in a certain way, which I was interested in analysing... Just as I sat around campfires in the evening with my native friends in the South Seas and participated in their feasts, so in Hollywood I had leisurely evenings with my friends, and went to some of their parties.' Powdermaker found that Hollywood people made excellent interviewees because their level of frustration was high and frustrated people love to talk. In all, she conducted some 900 interviews at the end of which process she concluded that Hollywood was indeed special. 'Hollywood is no mirrorlike reflection of our society, which is characterized by a large number of conflicting patterns of behaviour and values.' Instead, Hollywood had emphasized some of those values to the exclusion of others. Although Los Angeles was indisputably connected to the mainland, the natives persisted in regarding themselves as an island race.

Despite a local population that has always been renewed by fresh waves of immigration, from the East Coast, Europe and Latin America, the mentality of Los Angeles is that of a company town rather than a great urban metropolis. 'On some levels, Los Angeles is a one-industry town and everything tends to merge,' says Peter Benedek, a partner in the Beverly Hills-based talent agency, Bauer-Benedek. 'It's a small town once you come right down to it and you do run into people. People's kids tend to go to the same schools. People tend to live in the same neighbourhoods.' As is the nature

On days when the smog permits, you can see the Hollywood sign sandwiched between a perfect blue sky and a hillside dotted with matching swimming-pools.

of company towns, most movie people are exclusively preoccupied with what goes on within the city boundaries, despite the fact that the results of their work influence millions of people all over the world. When you live and work in Los Angeles it is easy to fall into the belief that your own little world is entirely confined within the range of the 213 and the 818 telephone prefixes.

But even that world turns. The city is constantly reinventing itself. Until very recently, downtown LA was a no-go area torn apart by gang warfare. Now the deco highrises are being bought up by the Japanese and the din of ambitious new construction drowns the cacophony of bumper-to-bumper traffic. And the natives emulate the rhythm of the city. Personal regeneration is more popular than ever before. Youth is at a premium and if exercise cannot slow the passage of time, then surgery, not always so subtle, can conceal its cruellest effects. Narcissism is endemic to Los Angeles. It's as if the entire city were absorbed in its own reflection.

The most popular sources of daily news in print are the trade newspapers – *Daily Variety* and the *Hollywood Reporter* – and, since the recent closure of the *Herald Examiner*, Los Angeles' one and only newspaper, the *Los Angeles Times*. Despite the sheer volume of its news coverage it sometimes seems like a third trade paper for the entertainment business in all but name. That the *Times*, like the entertainment business itself, is acutely sensitive to what its public needs is apparent in the bloated classified advertising section that makes it the most profitable newspaper in America. But it is less a window on the outside world than a mirror reflecting the city's own image back on itself. 'People who live in the Hollywood milieu are in a kind of cocoon,' says Michael Josephson. 'One gets an unrealistic sense of the rest of the world. I mean people read *Variety* rather than the *New York Times* for the most part, and therefore what's important are the ups and downs of an individual's career rather than what's going on in Eastern Europe. It is something that is quite noticeable once you invade that bubble from outside.'

Although he was born in Los Angeles, Terry Gilliam has chosen to work in Britain first as a member of the Monty Python team and then as a director. 'It's a surprisingly odd place. People don't have enough contact with the outside world,' he says. 'Everybody's sort of caught up in their own world. It's a tiny community that just feeds on itself. Very little of this place is based on real life experience.' His feelings are echoed by Martin Scorsese, the New York born director of *Taxi Driver*, *Raging Bull* and *Good Fellas*. 'It is a little odd to be in Los Angeles all the time where the main focus of every day is the film business. It's better if I separate from it. It's better for me to be in a city where maybe things aren't as affluent, where you can really concentrate on your work and not concentrate on which party you're being invited to and that sort of thing.'

Loretha Jones, a producer who was born in Harlem but spends much of her time in Hollywood, misses New York for what she calls her 'reality check'. In Los Angeles, she says, 'I might go to a party or a meeting and if we have a discussion about something, I'll say, "Well, what do you think about the breakdown of the Iron Curtain?" and people say, "Oh, is that a new band?" Here I feel very detached from what goes on in the world. People have to live real lives and here, Hollywood *is* their real life and it's scary because Hollywood is not necessarily real.' Because it revolves around the film industry, Los Angeles sometimes seems like a fabricated fairy tale world. When he is in Hollywood, John Boorman, the director of *Point Blank*, *Deliverance* and *Excalibur*, finds that his grip on reality is subtly loosened. 'The back lots of the studios with their Western streets, New York brownstones, Middle American main street, seem more solid than the suburbs surrounding them. As reality slips away, and unbearable lightness takes hold, you must hurry into a movie theatre and connect with a film. In LA, the shadows are more real than the substance.'

The screenwriter, Kurt Luedtke, keeps his distance. Despite his success with *Absence of Malice* and *Out of Africa*, he has resisted the temptation to move from Detroit to Hollywood. 'When I'm in Detroit I feel relatively affluent. When I get off the plane in Los Angeles, I immediately feel poor. I don't like that feeling so one way to deal with that is to just not get off the plane that often.' For some time, Luedtke has prescribed his occasional business trips to Hollywood by following a simple rule. A heavy smoker, he leaves LA for home as soon as he has exhausted a carton of cigarettes. 'If I did move to Los Angeles,' he says, 'I would start reading the trade papers, I would start going to lunches, I would start making up even more excuses than I have made up already for what to do on a given day that does not involve writing.'

Like Luedtke, Sam Cohn also chooses to live and work outside Los Angeles. Cohn is one of the most powerful agents in the business; his clients include Meryl Streep, Mike Nichols, Woody Allen, Sigourney Weaver, Lily Tomlin and many more. Cohn, a native New Yorker, is no fan of LA. 'It's a parochial place in which almost everybody is either in one business or related to it. You know, even the butcher and the doctor and so forth become satellites of the entertainment industry and I think it's a place where great temptation exists. The thing that most pleases me [about New York] is that I'm not in a mono-industry situation.' Like Kurt Luedtke, he has a system which minimizes the time he has to spend in Los Angeles. When business forces Cohn to visit the city, he makes sure he catches the 7.00 p.m. shuttle to LAX which arrives around 10.00 p.m.; he checks into his hotel and goes to bed; he does whatever work has to be done the next morning and then he takes the 4.00 p.m. flight back to New York.

But Kurt Luedtke and Sam Cohn are exceptional. For most people who work in the movies, it appears to be mandatory that they live in Los Angeles. 'This is a company town in no way different from

Agent Sam Cohn represents such big name talent as Meryl Streep and Sigourney Weaver but he spends as little time as he can in LA.

Silicon Valley,' says Dawn Steel, formerly president of Columbia Pictures. 'You have to live here to work here. I know very few people who have accomplished living outside the city and have been able to do the work they want to do. I think that it becomes very incestuous because your social life is so interconnected with your business life. All of my friends in Los Angeles are in the movie business or television or entertainment in some way.' For many, the pull of Hollywood is so insidious that by the time they are fully aware of it, it has become irresistible. Tim Harris is a young and successful screenwriter who, with his partner Herschel Weingrod, has penned a succession of commercial movies such as *Trading Places*, *Twins* and *Kindergarten Cop*. 'I think what happens is that if you are successful in Hollywood, you get paid so well that there is no way that your whole life is not going to change in every detail,' he says. 'Then once it changes, they've got you in a way. I was poor, and suddenly I'm upper middle class and I have a car and a house and if I want to maintain that, then I'd better keep working in the movies.'

As a company town, Hollywood is frequently compared with Detroit and the making of movies is often equated with the assembly-line manufacture of automobiles. But even in the forties, when the studios were churning out hundreds of movies a year, the analogy was misleading. 'It is illogical to carry the premises underlying the manufacture and merchandizing of automobiles to the making and selling of movies, because the problems involved are essentially different,' wrote Hortense Powdermaker. 'The product of the dream factory is not of the same nature as the material objects turned out on most assembly lines. For them, uniformity is essential; for the motion picture, originality is important. The conflict between the two qualities is a major problem in Hollywood.' It is questionable just how much importance Hollywood attaches to originality but the objection still stands. Detroit-based Kurt Luedtke is in no doubt that anyone who compares the making of movies to the making of cars in terms of an assembly line, knows very little either about making cars or making movies. 'If we made cars the way they make movies, we would all be pedestrians.'

There are much closer and more enlightening parallels to be drawn between Hollywood and another company town, Washington DC. In many ways, Los Angeles is a West-Coast sister-city to Washington. Gore Vidal, the writer and satirist, who has been closely acquainted with both worlds without ever entirely succumbing to the embrace of either, sees Washington and Hollywood as essentially the same place. 'I remember that when I first set foot in the Thalberg building in 1957 as a contract writer, one went down the corridor and you saw Christopher Isherwood, Aldous Huxley, Pandro S. Berman, and William Wyler, all in their little cubicles, and it reminded me of the White House, of the Executive Office Building with all the president's assistants working away.'

Washington, where the business is politics, and Hollywood, where the business is entertainment, have much in common. Both entertainment and politics are amorphous activities. Both require immense capital investment with which to generate results that are invariably transient and intangible. Both pursuits are highly speculative. Both have proven to be irresistibly attractive to gamblers and to those who desire to exercise power and influence over large numbers of people. Both are regarded with suspicion by the world outside. Both hold out the promise of immeasurable rewards for a chosen few. 'I've often thought as a reporter that working in Los Angeles and working in Washington were really the same job,' says Michael Cieply, a journalist who reports on the entertainment business for the *Los Angeles Times*. 'In Washington, everyone talks about inside the Belt. Here in Los Angeles, people talk about the Industry, the Town. The media come here with just about the same intensity as Washington. Every major United States publication, every major network has a presence. You report by all the same rules in Washington and Hollywood. I mean, I can't remember the last time I had an on-the-record conversation... And yet the heat is here. And it's that level of heat that sort of marries them. They're fascinated with each other. There's almost a shuttle that runs back and forth.'

Like politics in Washington, Hollywood's principal activity is a business of connections. Movie people are like so many spinning magnets, alternately attracting and repelling each other to a degree that can be bewildering. Contacts are born and nurtured at work and at play. The distinction between the two is often blurred. Meals, for example, at one of Hollywood's 'power restaurants' provide useful opportunities to 'network' and 'table-hop'. In a town which lives by the telephone, it is important to be visible at such occasions. Breakfast should be at the Polo Lounge in the Beverly Hills Hotel or at Hugo's canteen on Santa Monica Boulevard. Lunch should be at Le Dome on Sunset, 'the town's unofficial commissary' as producer Lynda Obst has dubbed it. And dinner should be at Morton's (Monday nights are best) or Spago's, famous for its pizza. Meals at these restaurants afford a chance to be seen with the right people, to let your fellow diners know what you are doing, or what you hope to be doing any day now, or at least to find out what they are up to. They are places in which to trawl for information and to spread gossip.

Hollywood is as inventive as Washington when it comes to conjuring up social events at which business can be conducted under the guise of leisure. Charity events compete to attract the big names because wherever the big names are, the medium-sized, small and minuscule are quick to follow. If you are on the list, a week is unlikely to pass without at least one invitation to a fund-raiser for some charity. 'All social life now is charity,' says actress Anjelica Huston. 'I get fifteen or twenty letters a day for everything from Yugoslavian dog illnesses to marathon diseases. It numbs you. So you write off a cheque for $20 to a charity to absolve yourself of guilt. It's a convent school of guilt.' Fund-raisers come in a variety of guises. It may be a premiere. It may be a salute to a star. It may be a theme party. The competition between charities is intense and the scramble to join the board of sponsors for the ones that really matter is akin to securing a seat on a Senate committee. Several of these charities were founded and are managed by people who truly care about the cause they sponsor. But charities also serve a political function. Much of the frenetic activity that surrounds these events is fuelled by self-interest. They are another venue in which to confirm or advance your status within the community.

A moment's respite from playtime.

One of the most desirable status symbols in Hollywood today is the possession of a pair of season tickets for court-side seats at the Forum. The Forum is the home ground of the Lakers, LA's local basketball team and, until recently, America's reigning champions. The games are entertainment extravaganzas complete with live music and Laker girls – from whose ranks the singer and choreographer, Paula Abdul, sprang to chart-topping heights – and an all-star cast of players. 'They're a studio chief's dream of a team: a seven-foot posse of good guys with a marked flair for the dramatic,' reported *Vanity Fair*. 'They're a box-office smash every time they play.' Most importantly, the Lakers are, or were until recently, not just winners but perennial winners, claiming the national basketball championships year after year after year. And Hollywood loves nothing more than a winner. As Lakers' fan Kirk Douglas says, 'Everybody loves a winner and nowhere more than in Hollywood where the vicarious thrill of identification with a winner might somehow rub off.'

The Lakers' games are Hollywood's equivalent to Ascot. Among the 17 500 fans, a choice selection of studio chiefs, stars, directors, producers and agents are conspicuous spectators, occupying the prized court-side seats. There are only 128 of them and on the black market they can go for as much as $3000 each for a single game. Jack Nicholson is a staunch Lakers' fan. He has become such a regular fixture that he is virtually a team mascot. When he films abroad, it is said that he has video tapes of every Lakers' game sent to him on location so he can keep in touch. It is impossible to quantify how much business is actually done here but during the play-off season almost anyone who is anyone in the entertainment business can be seen cheering on the home team. 'The Cannes film festival used to function the same way,' says Michael Cieply. 'The great thing about Cannes was you could go there and the studio chairman might talk to you like a regular guy. Now, the people who really count don't go to Cannes anymore. But Michael Ovitz of Creative Artists and Michael Eisner of Disney do show up at the Lakers' games. It's the one sure place where everyone who matters can be counted on to intersect. A lot of business gets done.'

Getting the business done, making the deal is what Hollywood is all about. When she was researching life inside the Dream Factory, Hortense Powdermaker was reminded of Lewis Carroll's *Alice in Wonderland*. 'It takes all the running you can do to stay in the same place,' she wrote. 'Always there is that struggle, for more and more of something, whether money, prestige, power, sensations, or what not, until the man drops dead. The game becomes the end, and is played compulsively.' Los Angeles is exactly the opposite of the laid-back, mellow melting pot of popular legend. The place is driven. The concentrated presence of so many desperate dreamers, the over-whelming ambition to score, makes you heady. Waiters and wait-resses who want to act; actors who want to be stars; chauffeurs who want to write screenplays; screenwriters who want to direct; delivery boys who want to be agents; agents who want to produce their own movies; producers who want to run studios; studio executives who dream of discovering some waiter or waitress who will be another Eddie Murphy, another Bette Midler.

CHAPTER TWO

CLAY FEET AND THE BOTTOM LINE

Not half a dozen men have been able to keep the whole equation of pictures in their heads.

F. Scott Fitzgerald

One of the things that you do when you become president of a studio is that you negotiate what happens when they fire you. Because eventually you will get fired.

Phil Alden Robinson, writer-director

Who's the boss? Who really runs Hollywood? Once upon a time that was an easy question to answer. Louis B. Mayer was the boss. Darryl Zanuck was the boss, as were Sam Goldwyn, Jack Warner, Adolph Zukor and Harry Cohn. In the thirties and forties these men ran the studios – the 'majors' as they were called – and the studios ran Hollywood. It was a feudal society. The studio boss was like a baron. He had absolute authority over the writers, directors, actors and producers under contract to the studio – the serfs and knights who owed obedience to their lord and who, in return, were granted protection. It is true that most of the old-style moguls were ultimately accountable to the 'suits' in New York. Louis B. Mayer reported to Nick Schenck, 'the *real* king of the pack,' as John Huston described him, who, as the president of Loew's Inc., quietly held the purse

Louis B. Mayer, the overlord of MGM, was finally accountable to his boss in New York.

strings of MGM. But New York was a long way away and on a day-to-day basis, the authority of the studio boss was absolute. Times change.

'In the days long gone,' says Richard Zanuck, 'there was never any question who was running Twentieth Century Fox. It was my father. I mean no one ever thought to question it. It never dawned upon anybody to think who would be running this company next week or next month. But now, there is always a question that whoever's in charge today, may not be there next week. That's completely different from the way it used to be.' Today, the top production jobs at the major studios are filled by a bewildering succession of executives who shift from company to company as if they were playing an elaborate game of musical chairs.

At Twentieth Century Fox, Zanuck's old stomping ground, the current studio chief, Joe Roth, is the fifth person to have the job in less than a decade. The same is true at Columbia Pictures where

Frank Price has begun his second tour of duty as chairman after resigning from the same job only six years earlier. Between bouts of Price, the studio had seen three separate regimes come and go in quick succession. Price's immediate successor was Guy McElwaine, an agent. He lasted three years. Then came David Puttnam, the British producer of such movies as *Chariots of Fire*, *The Killing Fields*, *Local Hero* and *The Mission*. Puttnam was out within fifteen months. He was followed by Dawn Steel, who joined Columbia from Paramount. She jumped ship two years later when Columbia's owners, Coca-Cola, sold out to the Japanese electronics giant, Sony. 'She did the best possible job she could in the time she had,' were the words Steel chose as her epitaph. The new owners, Sony, hired *Batman* producers, Peter Guber and Jon Peters, to manage their investment and they in turn hired Price to run the studio. 'It's not much different from the turnover rate in athletic teams,' says Art Murphy, an analyst for the entertainment trade paper, *Daily Variety*, 'but sports fans don't get too upset about turnover in General Managers. In fact, they demand it.'

All this is a far cry from the days when Zanuck senior held sway at Twentieth Century Fox. Zanuck's authority was founded on the studio's absolute control of the means of production and distribution. Fox was like a self-contained city state. Actors, writers, directors, producers, all the creative talent and labour that was required to produce a motion picture, signed exclusive long-term contracts to work for the studio. Darryl Zanuck would run his finger down the list of talent under contract to Fox – a list he kept pressed firmly on top of his desk beneath a heavy sheet of glass – and deftly put together all the elements necessary to make a movie. The studio also owned the sound stages, sets and all the facilities that went with their production. The studio distributed its own movies and effectively controlled their exhibition to the public through its ownership of the key first-run theatres. These were cinemas strategically located in

Darryl Zanuck kept a list of the artists on contract to Twentieth Century Fox pinned to his desk beneath a sheet of glass.

the major cities and towns which were the crucial sites for launching a new movie.

The studios built up and consolidated their power according to their ability to sell the stars who were under long-term contract to work for them. Next to the stars, who were the creation of the studios' marketing departments, it was the studios themselves who were synonymous with Hollywood. The Paramount mountain and the MGM lion were as potent a pair of icons of popular culture as Bogart's cigarette or Garbo's enigmatic smile. But from the mid-forties, the power of the studios went into decline and, like that cigarette and that smile, the appeal of their logos became largely nostalgic.

During the height of their powers, the studios monopolized the motion picture business. They controlled every aspect of the business from production through to distribution and exhibition. But in the late thirties, this monopoly came under scrutiny. In 1938 the Justice Department filed suit against the majors for restraint of trade. In 1948 a Supreme Court decision forced the studios to separate production and distribution from exhibition, and to sell off their theatres. At the same time the contract system began to collapse. The stars escaped and sought independent representation from talent agents. Actors, directors and writers were no longer conveniently on tap and the studios found themselves bidding for freelance talent in an

The birth of an icon: Leo the Lion is filmed for the MGM logo.

Richard Zanuck, son of Darryl and producer of the monster hit, Jaws, *and the more genteel Oscar winner,* Driving Miss Daisy.

increasingly competitive marketplace. Hollywood feudalism came to an end. The agents became more and more powerful and the men who ran the studios had to accept a new order in which they and the agents lived together in an uneasy relationship of mutual dependency. The shrinking powers of the studio boss were already well advanced by the time that Zanuck appointed his son to run production at Fox. In 1960 when the writer, John Gregory Dunne, spent a year studying the interior rhythms of the studio, he observed that it was virtually impossible for a production chief to put his personal stamp on a picture in the way that Darryl Zanuck had. 'He is, in many ways, a traffic manager, whose flexibility of action is far more limited than that of, say, the chief of an automobile company. Instead of assembling a "package" – story, talent, director, producer – he is more apt to be *presented* with one, take it or leave it.'

The studios were caught in a vice. Even as the costs of making movies were rising steeply, the market for them shrank as television and other pursuits claimed more of the public's leisure time. In America, cinema audiences plummeted from over 4000 million in 1946 to 820 million in 1971. The traditionally paternalistic studio management found themselves burdened with crippling overheads and mounting debts at the very time that interest rates were rising steeply. The studios slashed costs and sold off assets – the Twentieth Century Fox lot, for example, became the site for Century City's family of skyscrapers – but these expedients were not enough to save them. One by one the majors fell into the hands of corporate America: Universal to MCA, Warners to Seven Arts, United Artists to Transamerica Corporation, Paramount to Gulf and Western, MGM to the financier, Kirk Kerkorian. With few exceptions, the studios came under the control of men who might be able to read a balance sheet

The Twentieth Century Fox lot as it was under Zanuck.

but who had little instinct for the entertainment business. They employed others to run the studios on a day-to-day basis, men and women who were charged to perform quickly or suffer the consequences. Thus the studio boss became a disposable commodity.

Question: What's the last thing a movie executive says to his secretary as he leaves the office for lunch? Answer: 'If my boss calls, get his name.' Today, most studio bosses enjoy a professional life expectancy about equal to that of the fruit fly. Mel Brooks, whose production company has been housed on the Twentieth Century Fox lot for fifteen years, made a passing reference to how volatile the top job can be in his film about a Hollywood studio, *Silent Movie*. On the front of the boss's door was written the legend: CURRENT STUDIO CHIEF. 'The day you get the job is the day the clock starts ticking,'

The Twentieth Century Fox lot as it is today, overshadowed by Century City's family of skyscrapers.

says Brooks. 'You're doomed. I've seen armies of top executives come into Fox. I'm on the fourth floor and they're on the first and I look down every time the stock is sold and there is a change in administration. There's just a little blood and it soon dries off.'

Heads can topple for a variety of reasons. When a company changes ownership, the new landlords usually want their own people to run the show. When the Japanese electronics giant, Sony, bought Columbia Pictures in 1989 for a whopping $3.4 billion, it was 'sayonara' to the current incumbents – Dawn Steel and Victor Kauffman – and a warm 'ohayo' to a new team led by Peter Guber and Jon Peters.

Nothing sets the Hollywood rumour mills churning like a change of studio management. The cry, 'Out with the old; in with the new,' is rarely confined to the top dog and the effects can be devastating. Traditionally, the arrival of a new chief means a general bloodbath. Those executives appointed by his predecessor are thrown out or paid off with deals to make two or three movies for the studio as independent producers. 'Going indi-prod' is the accepted euphemism for putting ex-studio bosses out to graze although, in the volatile world of Hollywood, sometimes the grass in indi-prod land may be a great deal greener. Sherry Lansing has fared far better as an independent producer, making such hit movies as *Fatal Attraction*, *The Accused* and *Black Rain*, than she ever did as president of Twentieth Century Fox. Similarly, Dawn Steel shed few tears when she ejected herself from Columbia to become a producer. 'You don't resign from these jobs,' she said at the time, 'you escape from them.'

'Not a great many people want these jobs anymore,' says Ned Tanen, who is now an independent producer after more than a decade as a studio chief. 'There's too much money to be made in other areas of the business. Anyone trying to get into the ranks of

Dawn Steel shed few tears when she left her job as president of Columbia Pictures.

a studio executive looks around now and says, "Wait a minute. I can do a whole lot better as a producer." It's much easier to make more money, to have more freedom without being so totally wrapped up as an employee in an executive position.' Even so, the allure of the top spot persists and the musical chairs keep turning – 'The king is dead. Long live the king!'

The king may be dead but he leaves a legacy. The new studio boss automatically inherits a dozen or more films that have already been put into production by the previous regime. He may also find that he has been bequeathed a hundred or more projects that are in some stage of script development. Generally, those projects in development are put into 'turnaround' – they are frozen and offered for sale to other studios so that the development costs already incurred can be recouped. Finding yourself in turnaround is one of the more painful occupational hazards faced by writers, producers and directors who are trying to persuade a studio to bankroll some long-cherished project. Sometimes, if a screenplay has already been refined by several expensive rewrites, irrespective of its merit, it can become literally unfilmable. The script is loaded down with so many costs that potential buyers run for the hills rather than accept the debt.

And, although it should be in the studio's interest to ensure that the movies made by the previous regime make money, often the new boss and the attendant minions have little enthusiasm when it is time to distribute and market those movies to the general public. After all, what incentive do the new chiefs have when their achievement will be measured by the extent to which they can improve on the record of their predecessors? 'You can get really badly hurt,' says writer-director, Phil Alden Robinson. 'You could have the best project in the world, and if the regime changes, they tend not to

David Puttnam on location for Memphis Belle, *his first film as an independent producer after his brief stint at Columbia.*

give you the kind of support that you would like because they don't want to make the guy they replaced look good.'

Keeping the owner of the studio happy is no easy task, especially if the new studio boss is an outsider. When the British producer, David Puttnam, was appointed to run Columbia in 1986, he vowed to purge the movie business of the sin of excessive spending. He launched a crusade, denouncing agents and stars for inflating the cost of making movies because they demanded such high fees. But Puttnam stepped on the wrong toes. He rapidly found himself outmanœuvred by others who were far more savvy when it came to the intricacies of Hollywood politics. Within months, Puttnam had alienated a band of big names: Michael Ovitz, the powerful head of Hollywood's premier agency, CAA; producer, Ray Stark; stars, Warren Beatty, Dustin Hoffman, Bill Murray and, most significantly, Bill Cosby, America's number one television personality who also happened to own a healthy chunk of stock in Columbia's parent company, Coca-Cola. Puttnam was out within fifteen months. 'Hollywood eats outsiders for breakfast,' says attorney Peter Dekom. 'Hollywood does not want to change and since Hollywood is a town in which you have to get certain talent to work with you, if you come out alienating that talent, then I suspect the change you wish so very much to implement will never occur.'

But the single most important reason why so few executives stay on top for any length of time is that the movie business is driven by insecurity. The prime responsibility of the man or woman who runs a studio is to choose what movies the studio will make each year. And those movies have to make money. There are no particular qualifications for the job. Picking movies is not a science; it's an intuition, a gut instinct. It is generally accepted that people eventually make it or don't make it because they either do or do not have the knack. According to Ned Tanen, 'It's one of the last businesses in the world that is a seat-of-your-pants business.'

The pressures to perform are immense and the time in which you have to prove yourself is short. 'There's a lot of pressure to succeed instantaneously,' says Tom Pollock, president of Universal Pictures. 'So when somebody doesn't succeed instantaneously, there's often pressure to dismiss him or her before they have a chance to do what it is they set out to do.' It takes about eighteen months for the projects initiated by the new studio chief to trickle through the system and emerge as finished movies ready for release. If the new babies get a lukewarm welcome in the outside world then the boss's days are numbered. According to Tanen, 'You only need two or three expensive movies that don't do well within a given year, and your legitimacy is very suspect. Eventually you are going to lose because the odds are running against you.' Tanen managed to beat those odds by surviving as the chief of two studios – first Universal and then Paramount – for well over a decade, but few have approached his record. Sherry Lansing, the first woman to run a studio, lasted just three years as president of Twentieth Century Fox. 'It's a job that you can never really win at,' she says. 'The best thing you can hope for is a draw. You're only as good as your last film.'

When someone has a bad period picking movies, the studios – rather than understanding that there's no magic to it, that the power to pick the right movie could return as quickly as it left, rather than take that risk – will simply rotate one step to the right and put someone else in the job. According to Peter Dekom, whose stellar list of entertainment clients include among them the new Fox chief, Joe Roth, 'that's why studio executives make so much money. They don't expect to be in those jobs very long. They expect to be fired.'

Compared to the old-style moguls who were often part-owners of the company and who had the mentality of owner-entrepreneurs, the studio boss today is more likely to be a middle-level executive, an employee who is under pressure to perform very quickly or he will

Joe Roth, the new boss at Twentieth Century Fox, is the first film director to run a studio since Ernst Lubitsch ran production at Paramount in the thirties.

be replaced. Take Joe Roth, for example. He arrived to fill the top spot at Twentieth Century Fox Film Corp in the summer of 1989. Before joining Fox, Roth was a director-producer and a partner in the successful independent production company, Morgan Creek, which had made a bunch of low-cost hits, such as the brat-pack western, *Young Guns*, and the baseball movie, *Major League*. Both movies cost a little over $13 million to make and both made a big splash at the American box office. *Young Guns* grossed $44 million, *Major League* grossed $50 million. 'Joe Roth was brought into Fox specifically because he seemed to be able to make quality movies for less money,' says Dekom.

Roth is the first film director to take charge of a studio since Ernst Lubitsch ran production at Paramount in the thirties. But actually, what Roth is running is merely the movie division of a larger corporation, Fox Inc., which also owns the Fox Television Stations and the Fox Broadcasting Co. The chief executive of Fox Inc. is Barry Diller. He appointed Joe Roth. Although Roth has been given a large measure of autonomy, he is accountable to Diller, and Diller reports to the man who owns the company, the Australian-born press baron Rupert Murdoch. Fox, the movie company, had been performing poorly prior to Roth's appointment. In the summer of 1989, the studio gambled heavily and lost on an underwater, science-fiction thriller, *The Abyss*, which cost Fox some $50 million and returned less than half that at the American box office. It's still too early to tell if the new regime will succeed but Roth has been given an ambitious mandate to triple production to twenty or twenty-five films a year. And, says Diller, Roth has the right to put movies into production – to give them the 'green light' – without checking with him first. So far, so good, but Richard Zanuck is sanguine. 'As I understand it,' he says, 'Joe Roth has a deal in which he has total creative control. That may well be, but Joe doesn't own the company. Somebody else does. And there are people above Joe. So what I'm saying is, Joe should have that authority, there should be one voice, but if the one voice makes several mistakes in a row, no matter what the contract says, you know the ballgame will be over.'

Roth knows the score. 'There's a high turnover for these jobs because it's a hard job,' he says. 'It's like being the manager of a baseball team – you're expected to win.' A new studio boss generally enjoys a honeymoon period of about twelve to eighteen months. By then, the movies to which he's given the thumbs up will have started to trickle out to the theatres. What happens next is anybody's guess. 'There is no way of knowing what a movie is going to do,' says Tom Pollock, who admits that one of the toughest aspects of his job as president of Universal Pictures is waiting to see whether or not anybody is actually going to come and see one of his movies. 'We close our eyes and guess because there is no science to this. There is no way to predict anything. It's one of the joys and tribulations of the motion picture industry.'

Given the inherent insecurity of the business, it is no surprise that Hollywood is a superstitious community, or that it is especially susceptible to rumour. It may be impossible to predict a success but if the movie is likely to bomb, word often leaks out and spreads rapidly through town like some noxious gas. 'In most cases,' says Ned Tanen, 'people get a smell about a movie before it opens. It's this orphan that no one knows anything about. It's amazing how no one talks about it. Your friends don't talk about it. Your business associates don't talk about it. The guy who cleans your car doesn't talk about it. The Chairman of the Board doesn't talk about it. The only one who talks about it is the poor fellow in the accounting department, who has to figure out how he is going to write this damn thing off. He's talking about it to anybody who will listen.'

Of course, if you don't trust your own instincts you can always fall back on market research. Some studios test story ideas on the public to gauge the likely popularity of a given scenario. That such highly speculative audience research is even attempted shows how uncertain the studios really are when it comes to predicting public taste. But market research can be a dangerous expedient. According to Hollywood lore, one studio executive, within two months, put both *ET* and *Back to the Future* into turnaround because research told him that those movies would attract no one over the age of eight. 'I do not believe that the movie business is served by market research,' says Barry Diller. 'I think it should be abolished. It's a false totem pole. It does nothing except make people feel secure when they don't deserve to be.'

So it's back to instinct, gut feeling and luck. Those few studio executives who have enjoyed any longevity attribute their survival to little more than 'keeping their instincts clean', 'staying close to the audience' and making movies because they believe in them rather than trying to second-guess public taste. 'I have a great belief in what I like and I make movies based on that,' says Ned Tanen. 'I've never owned a screening room in my home. I don't go to private screenings. I pay to see movies and I go to the movies all the time. I rarely see any other studio executives at the movies. They just don't go. Instead, they go to someone's home for a screening or to a studio screening, which has nothing to do with an audience.'

Although market research is an unreliable tool with which to gauge the commercial appeal of a movie before it's made, all studios rely heavily on test screenings and polling techniques to try to assess the audience's response to a movie in progress and learn some lessons on how best to sell the movie once it's made. Research companies specialize in recruiting a representative selection of moviegoers who are then invited to see a preview – a 'sneak' – of the forthcoming movie. The response of the audience is carefully monitored and if the slightest signs of ennui are registered, the movie will be recut and tested again. The 'sneak' is the first opportunity for a studio to assess the public's reaction to a movie which may have absorbed years of effort and many millions of dollars. Most executives enjoy the experience almost as much as going to the dentist.

'It's so nerve-racking, it doesn't matter how many times you go through it. It never gets any easier,' says Dawn Steel, now the happily retired ex-president of Columbia Pictures. 'I know studio executives who have been through this hundreds of times and they still throw up.' Steel was president of production at Paramount when the studio found that their sample movie audience reacted badly to the last scene of *Fatal Attraction*, the thriller of marital infidelity starring Michael Douglas and Glenn Close. 'You heard the whispering,' she recalls. 'You heard the letting out of air, almost like they had been holding their breath for two hours and then the end was disappointing for them.' Paramount paid to have a new ending shot and substituted for the old one. *Fatal Attraction* went on to become the third highest grossing movie of 1987, generating more than $70 million at the American box office.

The pressures under which a studio boss has to function – the short-term need to succeed, the unpredictability of public taste, the rocketing costs of making movies and the consequent increase in the stakes at risk every time a movie goes into production – all combine to make the job, contrary to what you might expect, one of the least glamorous and most stressful in Hollywood. 'I retired at Universal in '82 because I was just burned out,' explains Tanen. 'The business just chews people up. It eats up all your time and all your energy and leaves you virtually no time in your life for anything else. It's a killing job.'

There are three key ingredients which make up the studio boss's job. Firstly, he or she has to decide what films to make. 'This is obviously the most important thing,' says Joe Roth. 'You can have the greatest hierarchy, and structure, and business plan in the world, but if you've made the wrong twenty decisions about what to put out, nothing can help you.' When Roth arrived to take the helm at Twentieth Century Fox, his immediate priority was to put together a production slate. With no movies being made, the studio was standing idle and the substantial costs of covering the overhead were mounting daily. The year prior to Roth's arrival, Fox had made only seven movies. Roth's mandate was to get production up to speed – his target was to triple the studio's output – so that Fox's distribution machinery could grind into motion as soon as possible.

The second function which the studio boss must fulfil is the distribution and marketing of the studio's movies to American cinemagoers. Studios are not merely production factories. They also distribute their movies through exhibitors – the cinema owners. In addition to putting out their own home-grown movies, studios also try to keep their distribution machinery fully occupied by releasing movies made by independent production companies. The studios charge a distribution fee for the movies they release, so when a studio-made movie is successful, they stand to make phenomenal profits both as a distributor and as a producer. For the studios, the domestic theatrical market – that's cinemas inside the United States – represents a prime launching pad for their product. Once a movie has established itself at home, it can be exploited more easily overseas. Maximizing the foreign exploitation of those movies is the third requirement of the studio boss's job.

The theatrical release of a movie is only its 'first run'. It is merely the first source of revenue, the first chance for the studio to recoup its investment. Beyond that, the movie will have up to four more runs in the so-called ancillary markets – ancillary, that is, to the theatrical market. The movie's second run is its release on video cassette. The video cassette market represents an increasingly lucrative source of cash. The movie's third run is on cable television or pay television, still an embryonic form of distribution in America, which requires a viewer to pay to see his or her chosen programme or film. The fourth run is network television. Finally, in the United States, the movie will be sold or syndicated to the several hundred local television stations.

The good news is that the market for movies is booming, not only in America but all over the world. In 1989, the biggest year in motion picture history, more than $5 billion was generated at the American box office, the third year in a row that box-office records had been shattered. More significantly, 1989 also set a new revenue record for video, now well established as *the* major revenue source for movies. At the beginning of the eighties, a studio's total receipts from movies broke down to 80 per cent from theatrical release and 20 per cent from the ancillary markets – video and television. By the end of the eighties, the theatrical portion had plummeted to 30 per cent and the ancillary markets accounted for a whopping 70 per cent of the movie's revenue. For example, in its first five months of theatrical release, Warners' blockbuster, *Batman*, grossed $250 million. When Warners released the movie on video cassette, *Batman* earned $400 million.

Even so, the importance of the theatrical release should not be underestimated. That's where the hits are made. In America, a major movie will be released simultaneously to well over a thousand theatres all over the country. The studio supports that release with a massive advertising blitz and as much promotional coverage in the nation's press and on television as it can muster. All this expense and effort is intended to maximize the movie's box-office returns in its opening weekend. Those weekend figures are crucial and studios are fond of taking out lavish two page advertisements in *Daily Variety*, trumpeting their latest movie's weekend gross. But although that weekend gross is important, a high opening figure does not guarantee that the movie will be a hit. To be a hit, a movie must sustain healthy figures over time. In Hollywoodspeak, it must have 'legs'.

'The response of the opening weekend's customers gives you the beginning of a clue as to how the movie will perform,' explains *Daily Variety*'s box office analyst, Art Murphy. 'If it does not open well, there is trouble ahead. If it opens very well, you don't know how far it can go, but at least you got it opened. The definition of a hit is something that runs and runs and runs and the success of a film depends on the word of mouth of the customers. Once you open the doors, it's the happy customer who makes it a hit. Some films have very big openings, but the word of mouth is bad, and they just disappear within a few weeks. But if a film is successful and catches on with the public, that establishes it as a hit. And the only place you can make a hit is in the theatres.'

Outside the United States, the growth in the demand for movies has been even greater. For example, revenues to the major American companies generated by the home video market in Japan, second in size only to that of the United States, more than doubled from $140 million in 1985 to $300 million three years later. And in Europe, the launching of a host of new television stations together with the building of new cinemas and a booming video market have meant windfall gains. Take the movie, *Willow*. Produced by George Lucas and directed by Ron Howard, *Willow* cost about $55.5 million to make and it went belly up at the American box office, returning a mere $27.8 million to the studio, MGM/UA Communications. But in addition to that, MGM/UA earned another $18.2 million from video cassette sales in the United States and $15.3 million from American television sales. Then add foreign earnings. Abroad, *Willow* generated $41.8 million in cinemas and another $21.7 million on video and television. All in all, the movie returned $124.8 million to the studio. Expanding markets. Booming business.

All the studios are rushing to increase their output and exploit the new opportunities. They're also enjoying an unexpected bonus in return for which they have to invest not one cent. Their libraries of 'golden oldies', accumulated over decades, and until recently regarded as virtually worthless, have been given a second lease of life by the arrival of all these new distribution outlets such as home video and cable and satellite television. It looks as if the studios are on the verge of a second Golden Age. Like veteran character actors written off before their time, they are making a comeback. Happy days are here again.

Of course, booming business is nothing new in Hollywood. The town was born and weaned on a series of booms and crashes. But the explosive demand for entertainment all over the world has generated a boom today that is quite unprecedented in its scale. However, the aphorism, 'Big is beautiful', applies not only to the newly enlarged marketplace for entertainment but also to the type of company that dominates those expanding markets. In Europe, Asia and America itself, companies in the entertainment business have been seeking to enlarge their market share by buying up or merging with their competitors. And companies that are not yet active in the entertainment business have been looking to buy into what they perceive as *the* growth business of the future. Today it looks as if the Hollywood studios are on everyone's shopping list irrespective of whether they *want* to be bought or not.

The closing years of the decade have seen a number of spectacular takeover bids, not always friendly, not always uncontested. They have thrilled the media and made some of the entertainment industry's chief executives almost as famous and just as rich as any movie star. In the closing months of 1989 two deals in particular hit the headlines: the merger between Warner Communications and Time Inc., and the purchase of Columbia Pictures by the Japanese electronics giant, Sony. Both deals were controversial. Both deals were an appropriate finale to a decade of spectacular mergers and acquisitions. Both deals were portents of the future, of the ways in which the entertainment business is likely to evolve during the nineties.

Take Steven J. Ross, the chairman of Warner Communications. In the words of *Fortune* magazine, money and controversy have followed him 'like stray cats in search of a meal'. Ross began his career selling women's bathing suits. Then he ran a chain of funeral parlours owned by his father-in-law. He branched out into limousine rentals and car parks. In 1962 he went public and seven years later he bought an ailing movie studio, Warner Brothers-Seven Arts. Bathing suits and funeral parlours may seem like an unlikely background for a Hollywood mogul but Ross thinks otherwise. 'I learned about people in the funeral business. It's a service business. You service people in an emotional time – you learn about their needs, their feelings.'

In a business where *who* you know is as important as *what* you know, Ross counts Clint Eastwood, Chevy Chase, Barbra Streisand and Steven Spielberg among his closest friends. Those longstanding friendships are very real assets to Ross's Warner Communications, a studio that has made its name on the profits of a string of movies which were megastar vehicles. However, success brings its own peculiar penalties and in 1983 Ross, who had built Warner Communications thanks to his own predatory instincts, realized that the company he founded was in real danger of being eaten alive.

When Rupert Murdoch wanted to diversify from his core publishing interests in Australia, Britain and America, he branched out into the entertainment business. He was looking to buy a studio and Warner Communications was number one on his shopping list. Ross was forced to take evasive action. He invited Herbert Siegal, the chairman and chief executive officer of Chris-Craft, to take a stake in Warners thus fending off Murdoch. But Warners' autonomy was bought at a high price for, although Ross retained control of the Warners board, he and Siegal were never comfortable with each other. Ross needed to bolster his position and guarantee the security of his company. Four years later, Ross set about securing those objectives in earnest. From 1987 to 1989 he devoted himself to negotiating the deal of a lifetime, one that would eventually result in the formation of the largest media conglomerate in the world.

The deal of a lifetime was the seemingly unlikely merger of

Rupert Murdoch's global media empire includes Sky Television in Britain and Twentieth Century Fox.

Warner Communications with Time Inc. Culturally the two companies were worlds apart. The corporate style at Time is Ivy League. The Warners people are flashy, streetwise highrollers. But the merger made sense. Time's video division, the phenomenally successful cable channel, Home Box Office, was generating more in sales revenue than its profitable but relatively stagnant publishing interests, which, besides *Time* magazine itself, included such publications as *Fortune*, *People*, *Sports Illustrated* and *Forbes*. Besides Time was as antsy as Warners when it came to safeguarding its own security.

Time's foreign competitors, the German media conglomerate Bertelsmann, Britain's Maxwell Communications Corp. and, most dangerous of all, Rupert Murdoch's insatiable News Corp. were all potential predators. On the thirty-fourth floor of the Time and Life Building, the senior management knew it was a case of eat or be eaten. Enter Steven J. Ross. On 4 March 1989, the merger, in the form of an acquisition of Warner Communications by Time Inc., was announced. Despite an attempt by Martin Davis, chief executive officer of Paramount Communications, to torpedo the deal, initially with a rival bid and then with a court action – *Fortune* magazine called the case 'the Super Bowl of corporate litigation' – the merger went through and a behemoth was born.

Just how big can you be and still be beautiful? As far as the newly minted Time-Warner goes, the answer to that question will only become clear with the passing of time. But one thing is certain. The era of mega-mergers, the formation of global media conglomerates will be the trend of the coming decade. 'We're competing with the multi-nationals of many, many countries,' says Ross. 'Entertainment is probably America's Number Two net export. Now we're Number One in that industry.' The rationale for being big is clear. The market today is a global market in which the launch of a movie creates a domino effect, the sale of a cinema ticket tripping the on-going sale of a series of related products. Movies and television shows are packaged and sold around the world, generating in their wake a host of spin-off merchandise – books, compact discs, T-shirts, posters and toys. Control of this market will fall to companies with the capacity to produce and market a family of related products on a global scale. When, shortly after the merger, Warners released the $35 million movie, *Batman*, the movie triggered the sale of video cassettes, record albums, compact discs and tapes, books and comic books – all items made by companies owned by Warners. It is too early to say whether the merger will work but the trend towards a global entertainment market is well underway.

The Time-Warner merger made front-page news. But no sooner had the story retreated to the inside pages than another tale from corporate Hollywood hit the headlines. The news that Sony, one of Japan's leading pioneers of high-tech hardware, had bought Columbia Pictures sent shock waves through the country. In Hollywood, the fact of the buy-out was no great surprise. It was widely known that Columbia's owners, Coca-Cola, were eager to back out of the company. Nor was it any great secret that Sony had been shopping for a studio for some time. But outside Hollywood, the deal tapped into a rising tide of xenophobia. It caused a massive furore.

Firstly, at that time Sony's purchase of Columbia Pictures was the largest takeover ever of an American company by a Japanese one. Secondly, Sony was buying a company in the entertainment business – America's second largest export earner – at a time when Japan was selling over $50 billion more in goods to the United States than America was exporting to Japan. Thirdly, Columbia was not just any old company. It was a pillar of American culture. Columbia's logo – the lady with the torch – was second only to the Statue of Liberty as America's dearest female icon. According to a *Newsweek* poll, 43 per cent of people surveyed about the Columbia purchase thought it a 'bad thing' and *Newsweek* found that 'more than half now consider Japan's economic might a bigger threat than the military power of the Soviet Union'.

It was richly ironic that Sony, which had always seen itself as a cosmopolitan corporate animal, should have caught the full backlash of American nationalism. In his memoirs, Akio Morita, the co-founder and chairman of Sony, noted that the name of his company had the distinct advantage of being meaningless in any language. 'In choosing our name,' Morita recalls, 'we did not purposely try to hide our national identity but we certainly did not want to emphasize it.' Sony had to become 'a citizen of the world'.

Sony established its name by specializing in audio and video hardware – radios, tape recorders, compact disc players, video recorders and cameras. Morita had pushed especially hard for his company to take the lead in video technology and it was Morita who coined the term 'time shift' to describe the ability of the Betamax video machine to record television programmes off-air for viewing at some later date. But the Betamax, pioneered by Sony and launched in America at great expense, was a rare and sobering flop. 'Time-shifting' became a way of life for millions of American television viewers but JVC's rival VHS video cassette format triumphed over Sony's Betamax. When the proud Sony customer trotted down to his neighbourhood video rental store, he found to his chagrin that there were far more titles available on the VHS format than on Betamax. So although Betamax technology survived as a specialist tool for professional broadcasters, it died as a consumer product.

The expensive failure of Betamax taught Morita a valuable lesson. The public will only buy an item of hardware, whether it be a video recorder or a compact disc player, if there is a sufficient library of software – movies or music – to play on the new technology. It is the desire to watch a movie or to listen to a piece of music together with its ready availability on a given format – video cassette or compact disc – that drives the consumer to buy the appropriate technology. Software drives hardware.

Morita put his experience into effect when he bought CBS Records in 1987 for the impressive sum of $2 billion. The deal gave Sony access to a generous library of musical talent, including Michael Jackson, Bruce Springsteen and Barbra Streisand among others. That library was not only valuable in its own right but was also, in Morita's judgement, indispensable to the successful launch of Sony's new compact disc player. The CBS Records purchase was a seminal event for Sony. It achieved everything Morita might have desired.

Akio Morita, the chairman of Sony, paid $3.4 billion to buy Columbia Pictures.

Sales of Sony compact disc players soared from 2.9 million machines in 1987 to 6.5 million in two years. Having established a model that worked in the audio field, the next step was to duplicate it in the video market. Morita saw two new Sony products, its 8 mm video cassette and its video disc, as the most promising consumer products of the nineties. He wanted the new formats to dominate the global market just as the video cassette recorder had been the dominant consumer product of the eighties.

After the Betamax debacle it was essential that Sony should be able to draw on an ample supply of movies to back up the sale of its 8 mm cassettes and video discs. 'After we acquired CBS Records,' Morita told *Newsweek*, 'I thought, "Now we have become the largest maker of music software in the world. And Sony is the largest video hardware company. So why don't we have video software?" Ever since, my mind has been set on making an acquisition in video software.' So shortly after buying CBS Records, Sony went shopping in Hollywood.

When Sony bought Columbia Pictures, with its library of over 2700 movies, it was not the first time that a Japanese company had invested in Hollywood. Sony's great rival, JVC, had already invested some $100 million in a new movie production company – Largo Entertainment – headed up by ex-Twentieth Century Fox boss, Lawrence Gordon. Inside Hollywood most observers were surprised less by the fact of the purchase than by the price Sony paid for the company and for the senior management Morita appointed to run it. Columbia Pictures was sold to Sony for $3.4 billion. Ever attentive to local sensibilities, Morita was careful to choose the right management and, as in the case of CBS Records, the right American management. Morita recognized that 'software people have special talents'. The final choice fell on Peter Guber. Guber, together with his partner, Jon Peters, was the hot producer of the moment. *Batman*, a Guber-Peters production, which had been financed and distributed by Warners, had notched up the highest box-office grosses in the studio's history – $450 million dollars worldwide. Just the year before, Guber and Peters had come close to running another studio – MGM – but the deal had collapsed at the last moment. Collaring Guber, and with Guber came Peters, to run their new studio seemed like a coup to Sony.

But there was a complication. Guber and Peters were under contract to Warner Communications, an exclusive five-year contract of princely generosity only recently consummated by the two producers and Steven J. Ross. As a result of the deal, Ross was looking forward to racking up heady box-office figures in the coming years from the *Batman* sequels, as well as forthcoming Guber-Peters' properties pledged to Warners, such as the movie adaptation of Tom Wolfe's best-selling *Bonfire of the Vanities*. Only months after the Time-Warner merger, Ross was not about to stand idle as his two most valuable producers defected to a rival studio. On 13 October 1989, just a couple of weeks after the Columbia purchase had hit the headlines, Warners filed a $1 billion breach of contract suit against Sony.

The Warners suit only added to the very real pressure in Washington to refer Sony's purchase of Columbia to Congress and this may have been a reason why Sony settled with Warners two days before the case came to court. The settlement terms were onerous. In return for releasing Guber and Peters from their contract, Warners extracted a host of hefty concessions. Sony agreed that Warners should have complete ownership of the jointly owned 144-acre Warner-Columbia studios lot in Burbank. Columbia would move to the old MGM lot in Culver City. Sony gave Warners a 50 per cent stake, worth between $225 million and $400 million, in the CBS Record Club, a valuable mail-order business. Warners secured the right to distribute Columbia's library of movies on basic cable television. And Warners retained the rights to all the properties developed by Guber and Peters including the *Batman* sequels, *Bonfire of the Vanities* and about fifty other projects. *Variety* estimated that the settlement cost Sony between $500 million and $700 million.

In addition, Sony bought out the Guber-Peters Entertainment Company for $200 million, nearly 40 per cent above its assessed market value, and agreed to pay the two executives each a base salary of $2.75 million a year for five years together with a healthy share of profits and 8.08 per cent of any appreciation in Columbia's assessed value. The terms were unprecedented in their generosity. All in all, Sony ended up paying almost $1 billion, 'a significant investment,' as *Variety* dryly put it, 'to staff Columbia with the managers of its choice.' Taking into account the $3.4 billion price tag for Columbia Pictures and the $1.4 billion in debt Sony agreed to assume, *Variety* calculated that Sony was shelling out about $6 billion for the privilege of owning a Hollywood studio.

The prevailing wisdom in Hollywood is that Sony overpaid for Columbia and its new management, but Sony takes a long and a broad view of its investment. Unlike the studio's previous owners, Coca-Cola, Sony has good reasons for being in the entertainment business and, unique among the other Hollywood players, Sony may even be able to bring down the costs of making movies by introducing new technology. Time will tell. Indeed, time is already beginning to do so. On Thursday, 22 November 1990, little more than a year after the Columbia buy-out, both Morita and his detractors were vindicated by an event which put corporate Hollywood back on the front pages of the nation's newspapers.

During its early years, Universal Pictures made its name on the strength of a string of cheap but effective horror movies. So it was appropriate that the board members of Universal's parent company, MCA, should have chosen to sell their business to Sony's great rival, the Matsushita Electric Industrial for $6.59 billion on the stroke of midnight. Matsushita may have paid more for MCA than Sony had paid for Columbia, but with its theme parks, prime real estate interests, a thriving music division and a proven management with an excellent box-office track record, MCA was generally considered a bargain buy at $66 a share. But if the MCA deal shows that Sony had paid a premium price at a time when the market was peaking, it also confirms Morita's good judgement in buying into Hollywood. It looks like Steven J. Ross and Akio Morita have set a trend, and one which has had an immediate effect on Hollywood's own working practices.

'I think that an extraordinary change has happened over the last five or six months because of the Sony acquisition,' says Dawn Steel, who resigned from Columbia in the wake of the buy-out. 'Every studio head in town renegotiated his deal after that acquisition happened. And the actors turn around and say, "Well, if they're worth $200 million, what am I worth?" What's Eddie Murphy saying? What's Arnold Schwarzenegger saying? What's Sly saying? And I think that trickles down to the directors and the writers.'

Reporting on Hollywood's reaction to the deal Sony struck with Guber and Peters, the *New York Times* headlined its story, 'On Feeling Underpaid at $1 Million'. The *Times* went on to detail how, as a result of Guber and Peters' unprecedented compensation, Hollywood's salary structure was beginning to crumble: 'The statement repeatedly heard around town last week was that if Mr Guber and Mr Peters are worth the kind of money Sony is paying, Tom Pollock who has turned Universal from an also-ran into a frontrunner, must be worth $850 million, and Jeffrey Katzenberg, who changed Disney from a backwater into Hollywood's No. 1 studio last year, must be entitled to more than a billion dollars.' According to the *Times*, the compensation for Guber and Peters is changing the nature of the business.

Executive salaries are not the only cost increases that are rocking Hollywood to its foundations. Prices for stars, writers, directors and on down the line to cinematographers and editors are rising fast. The services of Richard Donner, director of the buddy thriller, *Lethal Weapon*, can now be had for a $4-million fee and a share of the box-office gross. James Cameron, who directed the hit science fiction thriller, *The Terminator*, is getting $6 million to direct a sequel. Arnold Schwarzenegger earned a $10-million fee to star in the futuristic thriller, *Total Recall*, and Sylvester Stallone was paid more than $20 million to reprise the title role in *Rocky V*.

'The cost is so astronomical now,' says Ned Tanen, 'the risks are so great that it's more and more difficult to put movies together.' Today a major film starts at $23.5 million, a 40 per cent increase since 1985. On the back of that you start putting on the marketing costs, which can easily be $15 million or $20 million, probably more. 'You're talking about the gross national product of most African nations,' says Tanen. Then you have to factor in the interest on that cash – another few million dollars – together with the overhead costs of running the studio and the distribution operation. To make back its money, a movie has to return upwards of between $50 million and $60 million to the studio. That doesn't happen very often. A blockbuster like *Batman* or *Lethal Weapon* might do that and more, but the profits from those movies, both of which were made by Warners, have to offset the losses the studio sustained on the dozen or more other movies it released that year.

The costs of making and marketing movies have gone, in the words of Barry Diller, 'from simply crazy to rollickingly insane'. One reason for the skyrocketing prices is that the people who make the films, the talent and the technicians, know how much money the studios are making from the ancillary markets. It's a question of supply and demand. The studios are desperate to make as many movies as they can, as fast as they can, to exploit the booming market. They're falling over themselves to buy commercial scripts and sign up hot directors and stars. But there's only so much talent to go around. 'The motion picture business is a business that Adam Smith would recognize,' says Tom Pollock. 'It follows capitalism as set down in *The Wealth of Nations*, a book written two hundred years ago. Individuals sell their services to the highest bidder. When there is a lot of money chasing a small amount of talent, prices go up. Everybody's prices are inflated.'

Right now, it's a seller's market and the brokers who sell the talent – the agents – are only too happy to exploit the studios' hunger and extract top dollars for their clients. 'Hollywood is a place full of scared people,' says Alex Ben Block, editor-in-chief of *Show Biz News*, a weekly newsletter. 'It's less scary to make a $50-million film than a $10-million film. For $50 million you can afford big stars and special effects and you know you'll get some money back – even if it's only on video-cassette sales. With a $10-million film with no stars, you run the risk of losing it all.' Studios can try to protect themselves by developing projects in-house rather than relying on the agents to present them with the fully formed package of script, star and director neatly tied up together. And they can also try to hedge their bets by offering the star or director a share of the box-office takings in return for a modest payment upfront. This is what Tom Pollock did when he put together the elements to make the comedy, *Twins*. The two stars, Arnold Schwarzenegger and Danny DeVito, and the director, Ivan Reitman, took no fee for their services. Instead they received a percentage of the profits. 'They gambled on the movie,' says Pollock, 'and because the film was very successful they made a great deal more money than they would have made had they taken cash and less of a back-end.'

But, as Tom Pollock admits, in the last resort, 'There's not a whole lot you can do about the prices of the actors if they are the actors you want to work with.' As long as the studios compete so fiercely to attract the best scripts and the biggest stars, the agents are well placed to jack up the prices. Producers often blame agents for the runaway inflation that's hitting movie costs, but ultimately it's the buyers, the studios, who are responsible for their own lavish spending sprees. 'Agents are not to blame for the cost of movies,' says Barry Diller. 'The only people to blame for the cost of movies are the people who run the movie companies. No one else.'

Whenever a star, a director, a screenplay or a book is perceived

suddenly as something that everybody wants, you have a feeding frenzy. Everybody wants to hire that person or acquire the rights to that screenplay or book. That of course shoots the price up. If a new all-time high price is paid for an original screenplay, it reverberates all the way down the line so that second, third and fourth level quality screenplays can command higher prices. And if a writer sets a new price peak, that prompts the directors and the stars to reassess their own fees. This makes levering a movie off the ground an increasingly expensive proposition. And once production gets underway, costs can easily spiral out of control. The bigger the budget, the greater the potential margin for error.

Industry tongues were set wagging when it was revealed that Bruce Willis, a television star with no track record on the big screen, had been paid a whopping $5 million to star in the Twentieth Century Fox thriller *Die Hard*. The movie did well and when Joe Roth arrived to take command at Fox, one of his first production decisions was to set a sequel in motion. But, according to the *Wall Street Journal*, costs on *Die Hard II* rocketed to almost $60 million. *Days of Thunder*, which comes from the same team that made the mega-hit, *Top Gun* (director Tony Scott, star Tom Cruise, and producers Don Simpson and Jerry Bruckheimer) is said to have cost Paramount upwards of $50 million. 'There's an enormous loss of control over spending,' says Barry Diller, 'and the repercussions will be bad. Who is going to get struck by the lightning, where and how, I can't tell you. But the loss of control is almost all-pervasive. There is a whole slew of pictures with budgets above $40 million. Some of them are going to lose a lot of money.'

The movie business has always operated in cycles which have

Universal Pictures' Tom Pollock gave up a hefty share of the box office on Twins *in order to get the stars he wanted, Arnold Schwarzenegger and Danny DeVito.*

lasted for about three and a half years. If past records are anything to go by, the market growth that has distinguished the last few years should be tailing off fairly soon. 'The only thing that is going to stop the acceleration of production and marketing costs,' comments *Daily Variety*'s Art Murphy, 'is when these newer markets reach saturation and there are no new markets on the horizon. That's the only thing that is going to bring costs into line.' The repercussions could be devastating.

Barry Diller thinks the movie business is on dangerous ground because its fixed costs, its production costs, its marketing costs have become so huge that the studios need everything churning along fairly rapidly to be able to recoup. And if any of the markets which have expanded greatly over the last ten years get hurt – if for instance there is a recession in the video market in the United States – then the studios will face a major crisis. 'If there is this crisis,' says Diller, 'then you'll see an immense amount of blood on the floor.'

Barry Diller believes that mushrooming costs mean the movie business is on dangerous ground.

Will it all end in tears? A sharp, painful crying jag is more likely. Hollywood has faced and survived downturns before. And should larger problems loom – a ballooning national deficit or recession in the world economy – then the movie industry can console itself with the thought that in the past it has proven itself to be remarkably resilient to such events. During the Great Depression, when Wall Street was speckled with the bodies of suicidal bankers and the country starved, the movie business was blooming. Hollywood has always thrived on people's need to escape into entertainment, and their appetite for movies seems to endure through bad times as well as good. The studios will survive. Only the names of the men and women who run them, and the companies that own them, are liable to change.

CHAPTER THREE

HEAVENLY BODIES

I have a theory that the camera likes some people ... and the people it likes can't do any wrong.

Howard Hawks, director

Today, a million dollars is what you pay a star you don't want.

William Goldman, screenwriter

Stars sell movies. Those three words have been the mantra of moviemakers for almost as long as movies have been made. The audience's allegiance, no matter how fickle, to a handful of blessed actors is one of the few seeming certainties in a business of chance. At least that is the thought with which Hollywood executives console themselves as they sign the multi-million dollar cheques to a star who, as often as not, needs them far less than they need him or her. Of course, nothing and nobody, not even the most popular of stars can guarantee absolutely that a movie will sell. But the fact remains that stars are the best insurance policy going. Lavish production budgets are no guarantee that the movie will succeed. Neither the wittiest of writers nor the best of directors can ensure a hit. Special effects won't get you there. And no Hollywood studio can sell a movie on the strength of its name.

The Warners' shield, the MGM lion, the Paramount mountain might evoke a certain amount of nostalgia among moviegoers, but studios cannot brand-name their movies in the same way that Coke and Pepsi brand-name their soft drinks. Only stars can come closest to doing that: Stallone in *Rocky* or *Rambo*; Schwarzenegger in *The Terminator* or *Total Recall*; Cruise in *Top Gun* or *Cocktail*; Murphy in *Beverly Hills Cop* or *Coming to America*. All those movies have two characteristics in common. They were all monster hits and each one of them owes its commercial success to the presence of a *bona fide* box-office star whose name on the cinema marquee brings with it brand-name recognition irrespective of whether the movie happens to be any good or not.

To the moviegoing public, stars may signify icons of a bygone age, or heroes and heroines who may release us momentarily from the drudgery of everyday life, or unattainable lovers, or people whose performances simply inspire us. Many of us might number Robert De Niro or Meryl Streep or Robert Duval among today's greatest stars. Not in Hollywood. There, the men and women who work the numbers have their own pantheon of stars, and De Niro, Streep and Duval are not among them. They may be great actors but stars they are not. 'A star has two things that an actor doesn't have: charisma and the ability to sell tickets,' says Ned Tanen. 'Eddie Murphy will sell tickets around the world to a movie that is not a very good movie. That is a movie star. Robert De Niro is a great actor. He doesn't necessarily sell tickets. When you pay an Eddie Murphy or a Tom Cruise or one of that handful of people, you are paying someone who brings something to the movie. It means something to an audience. They're interested. Their antennae go up. They may not like the movie; the movie may not be successful, but they will get it opened.'

In Hollywood, a star is defined as an actor who can 'open' a movie. 'Opening' a movie is Hollywood lingo for the ability to entice sufficient numbers of people who will pay to see the movie during its first weekend, sufficient, that is, to merit the placing of a double-page, full-colour advertisement in *Daily Variety*. The studios traditionally trot out their summer blockbusters between the beginning of June and the end of August and each week *Daily Variety* will be speckled with advertisements trumpeting the weekend grosses of the latest releases. During the summer of 1990 a succession of such advertisements celebrated the opening grosses scored by Tom Cruise in *Days of Thunder* ($21 502 162 over five days), Eddie Murphy in *Another 48 Hours* ($19 470 596 over three days), Michael J. Fox in *Back to the Future, Part III* ($23 703 060 over four days), and Arnold Schwarzenegger in *Total Recall* ($25 533 700 on its opening weekend). Bruce Willis in *Die Hard II* also scored high. *Daily Variety* pegged the movie's first weekend at between $22 million and $25 million.

The studio bosses who have invested between $30 million and $60 million in what they hope will be that summer's big movie, pore over those opening weekend figures with the feverish curiosity of men who know that they are reading a prognosis of their own careers. The screenwriter William Goldman has famously said of movie people that 'Nobody knows anything'. But everyone in Hollywood knows what sells a movie. It's called 'word-of-mouth'. If a friend recommends a movie the odds are pretty good that you will act on that recommendation. That's word-of-mouth and nothing is more certain to put a spring into the stride of a studio executive than the news that his or her latest movie has good word-of-mouth.

The problem is that good word-of-mouth cannot be bought at any price and bad word-of-mouth is every studio boss's worst nightmare. It is lethal to the movie's chances of box-office survival. However hard a studio might hype a movie, once the house lights dim, that movie has to sell itself. If the audience doesn't buy it then the word-of-mouth can be devastating. Studios try to hedge their bets by test-screening movies. A research company will recruit a representative audience, usually at a shopping mall, and then monitor the audience's response using standard questionnaires. Depending on the results, the movie might be sent back to the editing room for some judicious recutting. But irrespective of the test-screening, the opening weekend is always a tense time for the studio, especially if the movie has cost an arm and a leg to make. Small, inexpensive movies can afford to open in a few theatres and wait around until word-of-mouth builds up. But big movies, which can absorb as much money to market as they cost to make, cannot afford that luxury. They need good word-of-mouth and they need it now. In order for that to happen, the studio needs to establish a critical mass of support for the movie during its first few days in release. That means that sufficient numbers of people must turn out to see the new movie during its opening weekend.

Studios try to boost the opening weekend figures of a new movie in a variety of ways. One way is to spend alarming amounts of advertising money. Another way is to have a concept that is so generically accepted that if you make the movie, people will come. *Teenage Mutant Ninja Turtles* is a good example of this. Based on a best-selling comic strip, the movie was one of the monster hits of 1990. And it had no stars in it. Nevertheless it is the accepted wisdom in Hollywood that your safest bet by far is to engage the services of a star. 'If you want some security about making a $30 million investment, it would be very nice to have Danny DeVito or Michael Douglas or Robert Redford on the other end of that camera,' says Joe Roth. Shortly after becoming the new chairman of Twentieth Century Fox, Roth took out his own insurance policy by signing Bruce Willis to star in the sequel to the studio's 1988 hit, *Die Hard* Roth admits that signing a star 'doesn't mean necessarily that people will come to the film', but without Bruce Willis *Die Hard II* would never have been made. With Bruce Willis not only was the movie made – at a cost of some $60 million – but when it was released it promptly hit the Number One spot on *Daily Variety*'s weekly box-office chart. Bruce Willis got the movie opened. Good word-of-mouth did the rest.

If the financial history of Hollywood stardom were ever to be written, Bruce Willis would merit a meaty footnote. Five years ago, Willis was not a movie star. He was big in television as the co-star of the tongue-in-cheek detective series, *Moonlighting*, but his attempts to cross over to the big screen had come to nought. Then came *Die Hard*. Twentieth Century Fox was committed to making the movie and the studio had made elaborate preparations to go into production. But with only weeks to go before the start of principal photography they had failed to sign a star. All the big names were either unavailable or just not interested. Enter Jake Bloom, a leading entertainment attorney who wears his hair long and favours the casual macho clothing that complements his client list, which includes Arnold Schwarzenegger and Sylvester Stallone, the kind of people for whom the Fox executives would have gladly sold their grandmothers. Schwarzenegger and Stallone were not for sale but another of Bloom's clients, Bruce Willis, was.

The Fox executives were desperate and Bloom persuaded the studio to take a gamble. Although Willis had no track record at the box office, and there was no evidence that he could sell a movie, Fox agreed to pay him $5 million to play John Maclean, the hero of *Die Hard* and the nemesis of any international terrorist who might be foolhardy enough to pass through LA. The Bruce Willis gamble almost didn't pay off for Fox. *Die Hard* did well but not spectacularly at the American box office. But its 'afterlife' – Hollywoodese for a movie's second run on video cassette – was phenomenal. *Die Hard* sold exceptionally well on video, so at the end of the day it was a smash success. But the important fact about *Die Hard* was not the question of whether or not it would make a profit for the studio. The important fact was the Bruce Willis deal. It set a marker. Willis was not a star but if he was getting $5 million, what was Schwarzenegger worth? Agents went scurrying back to their calculators and a chill settled over the executive offices of the studio bosses. Things would never be the same again. 'Five years ago someone making $5 million for a movie was virtually unheard of,' says Jake Bloom's partner, Peter Dekom. 'Today it's not unheard of for someone to make $10 million to $15 million for a single film.' By the time Fox got around to making a sequel to *Die Hard*, $5 million for Bruce Willis looked cheap. During the interim, star salaries had shot through the stratosphere and into hyperspace.

Of course, Bruce Willis, Jake Bloom and the executives at Twentieth Century Fox cannot claim all the credit for sending costs spiralling skywards. Today, it's a seller's market in Hollywood. Movies are bigger business than they have ever been. Cinema ticket sales in America surged from $4.64 billion in 1988 to $5.02 billion in 1990. Video cassettes and sales of movies to the American television networks added another $3.37 billion and $1.7 billion respectively to the studios' coffers. And, around the world, American movies released in 1989 brought in revenues totalling $11.6 billion – an increase of 100 per cent compared with the figures achieved five years before. According to entertainment analysts, total worldwide earnings could hit $19.2 billion by 1994. As studios and producers rush to get their pet movies into production to take advantage of a booming market, the competition to sign up star names is intense.

The studios are prepared to pay high prices for stars but they often find themselves bidding against a select band of independent companies who are happy to pay even more than anybody else. Unlike the studios, the independent companies do not distribute the movies they make so they do not have to finance the costs of running an expensive distribution operation too. Instead they finance their movies by securing big cash guarantees from local distributors around the world in advance of the movie going into production – the so-called pre-sales technique. Then they sell the domestic distribution rights – the right to release the movie through cinemas in the United States – to one of the studios, who are always desperate for product to keep their marketing and distribution departments busy. By making lucrative distribution deals in foreign markets, an independent company can be well into profit before the cameras start turning. But in order to pre-sell a movie that doesn't yet exist to a distributor in France or Germany or Taiwan, the production company needs to provide some insurance that the movie has a more than average chance of commercial viability. That means selling the movie on the basis of a star name.

Carolco Pictures, which is one of Hollywood's most successful independent companies, has made millions by pre-selling movies such as *Rambo*, *Red Heat* and *Total Recall* on the names of Sylvester Stallone and Arnold Schwarzenegger. Carolco spent almost $60 million making the science-fiction extravaganza, *Total Recall*, but the company's president, Peter Hoffman, maintains that thanks to Schwarzenegger's name they were able to cover those costs through pre-sales well before they went into production. He expects *Total Recall* to bring in more than $300 million in foreign revenues.

'We make movies that compete with the major studios in the international market,' says Carolco's vice-president, Thomas Levine. 'They have to contain a big element – like Arnold or Sly or Mel Gibson. That is what lets us compete. So there's not that much quibbling about salaries.' Carolco paid Arnold Schwarzenegger a $10 million fee to star in *Total Recall*. Studio bosses like to blame companies like Carolco for inflating star salaries. Ned Tanen is in no doubt that the independents just throw money out of the window because they are desperate to attract serious talent. 'They will give somebody 25 per cent more, 50 per cent more than that person has ever made just to get their name on the roster. Well, once that price has been established, it's been established. It just keeps escalating.' But with Carolco riding high on the profits it makes from movies like *Total Recall*, it's unlikely they will scale down the level of their bidding. Just weeks after *Total Recall* opened, the company paid a

According to Dawn Steel, $7 million for Mel Gibson is a bargain. 'I am sure he is up to around $10 million by now, maybe even more.'

record $3 million for a new script called *Basic Instinct* by Joe Eszterhas. Michael Douglas has been signed to star. His fee is said to be $15 million.

'Deciding how much money to pay a star is probably one of the most difficult decisions there is to make and also probably one of the most anxiety-causing decisions,' says Dawn Steel, a former president of Columbia Pictures. 'I remember when it wasn't so long ago that Mel Gibson's agent told me that he wanted $7 million for him. Now I didn't have to make that decision because Mel Gibson was not ready to commit to the particular movie that I wanted him to do. But as it turns out, $7 million is a bargain for Mel Gibson, because I am sure that he is up to around $10 million by now, maybe even more.'

As long as the supply of stars who can open a movie is relatively small, and the demand for those stars is overwhelming, then it's a matter of simple economics that their prices are going to go up.

Simple economics dictates that Sylvester Stallone, for example, gets $20 million for his work in *Rocky V*. In fact, Hollywood stars are making so much money these days that they can afford to share some of the risk with the studios. Instead of taking an upfront fee, some stars opt for a share of the movie's earnings. As a demonstration of their unprecedented power in Hollywood today, the stars have become partners with the studios.

If the terms of the deal work out then everybody's happy. Universal's blockbuster comedy, *Twins*, made more than $110 million at the American box office and only cost the studio $18 million to make. That's because the two stars, Arnold Schwarzenegger and Danny DeVito, together with the director, Ivan Reitman, took a nominal salary upfront in return for a share of the studio's gross profits. When the time came to divvy up those profits – which worked out at about 40 per cent of the box-office take – Universal had to stand in line behind Schwarzenegger, who took a 17.5 per cent share, DeVito and Reitman. For reprising his role in *Ghostbusters II*, Bill Murray earned an upfront fee of only $25 000 but his 15 per cent share of the gross made him millions more. In that instance, the studio, Columbia Pictures, had to wait until not only Murray, but also co-stars Dan Aykroyd, Harold Ramis and director Ivan Reitman had subtracted their cuts. All in all, Columbia Pictures president, Dawn Steel, gave up 45 per cent of the movie's earnings to the principal participants in order to get *Ghostbusters II* into production at a reasonable cost.

This is not a new phenomenon – in 1950 James Stewart's agent, Lew Wasserman, made a deal with Universal whereby Stewart waived his customary fee of $250 000 in return for a half-share in the net profits of the movie, *Winchester '73* – but current proponents of the so-called 'back-end' deal have added a new spin to the old formula. Today, some stars share the profits without sharing the risk – they get to have their cake and eat it too. Warner Brothers, for example, agreed to pay Jack Nicholson a hefty upfront fee – $7 million – to play the over-the-top villain, the Joker, in *Batman*. In addition to that, Nicholson took home a 15 per cent share of the gross. And Arnold Schwarzenegger commanded the same 15 per cent gross share in *Total Recall*, as well as the $10-million fee Carolco paid him upfront.

The lengths to which a studio will go to retain a top star were revealed publicly when the writer and humorist Art Buchwald sued Paramount Pictures for withholding profits that he alleged were due to him and his producer from the movie, *Coming to America*. It was a landmark case in several respects. Paramount was forced to open its books in court and the Byzantine accounting methods of a Hollywood studio, which are normally shrouded in secrecy, were revealed to the outside world. Documents submitted by Paramount

One-third of Coming to America's *$39-million budget went to Eddie Murphy Productions.*

to the court and subsequently extracted in *Daily Variety* showed that approximately one-third of the movie's $39-million budget went to Eddie Murphy Productions. Of this amount, Murphy received $8 million to star in the movie, $200 000 in the form of a writer's fee and $500 000 as part of his 'producer's package'. Another $1.75 million was added to the cost of the movie to cover Murphy's 'overhead'. This actually related to a 'sweetener' of $6.8 million which Paramount had paid Murphy in the form of a re-signing bonus to enter into an exclusive five-picture deal with the studio. In addition, Paramount charged another $1 million against the movie to cover miscellaneous expenses incurred by Eddie Murphy and his entourage. These expenses included $115 000 for Murphy's limo and driver, $60 000 for travel and hotel accommodation for his staff, and $90 000 for Murphy's cost-of-living allowance. 'Even by Hollywood's standards,' said Buchwald's attorney, Pierce O'Donnell, 'the amounts spent are obscene.'

The studios would claim they have no choice but to pay up. Before the lacklustre box-office performance of *Harlem Nights*, Eddie Murphy had an impeccable track record. It seemed he could sell any movie, no matter how bad it was. But there is only one Eddie Murphy. 'There aren't very many movie stars,' says Ned Tanen. 'There are a lot of people who are paid like movie stars but there are really only half a dozen movie stars in this world and it is very difficult to get them to work. Since we are no longer living in the wonderful contract era of the twenties and thirties and forties, you don't *own* these people. They don't *have* to do your movie. You are trying to put the best ingredients together and if they turn you down, your choices get more and more limited. So you put the best people you can into it and then you may find yourself paying three, four, five million dollars to people who, frankly, their mother won't pay to see them in a movie. In many cases you are overpaying for what you are getting but you end up talking yourself into going with these people, who may be incredibly gifted actors and actresses, *but they don't sell tickets.*' If a studio can't get their first, second or third choices they may have to take a chance on an unknown name. But after the *Die Hard* deal set a precedent, even the lack of any prior box-office clout doesn't necessarily mean that studios save money upfront by opting to cast an unproven actor.

Of course, money cannot buy you everything and paying a star tens of millions of dollars does not always mean the movie will be a hit. Even the track record of box-office behemoths like Stallone, Schwarzenegger, Murphy and Cruise does not mean that any star can sell any movie. Brand-name recognition can sometimes turn against a star when the movie fails to cater to the audience's expectations. The commercial fallibility of even the biggest box-office performers is a fact of life that studio bosses are reluctant to admit. It's considered bad karma to bring up these freakish duds. It makes studio people queasy. They turn coy. Mention *Rhinestone* to a studio executive who has just put his or her job on the line to back Sylvester Stallone as a romantic lead and watch the conversation keel over and die. Stallone may have hit the jack-pot with a string of macho roles spawned by *Rocky* and *Rambo*, but when he paired with Dolly Parton in the romantic comedy *Rhinestone*, audiences stayed away in droves. Same story for the prison drama *Lock Out*, another movie where Stallone's name above the marquee had about as much audience appeal as nuclear waste. Ditto Warren Beatty and Dustin Hoffman, who were of little help to Columbia Pictures when the studio tried to recoup the $45 million which had been spent on the box-office dud, *Ishtar*.

Stars are only human. They make mistakes. And the studios will tolerate these mistakes, even if it costs them millions of dollars, but only up to a point. Take Richard Gere, for example. In 1982, Gere was one of Hollywood's hottest leading men. Four years later his dismal track record at the American box office threatened to capsize

Sylvester Stallone Mark I in Rocky, *and Mark II (the new improved model with added intellect and humour) in* Tango & Cash.

his career altogether. No sooner had Gere become Hollywood's darling on the strength of his success in *American Gigolo* and *An Officer and a Gentleman*, than he went on to make a string of spectacular flops including the $51-million gangster movie, *The Cotton Club*, and a forgettable biblical epic, *King David*. At that point the word on Gere was that he couldn't get himself arrested. Then his luck changed. In 1989, Gere's agent, Ed Limato, suggested he take a chance by playing a villain in a slick, sinister thriller called *Internal Affairs*. The movie was a success and Gere's performance as a corrupt city cop went some way to reviving his career. A month or so later, he played the romantic lead in *Pretty Woman*, a comic reworking of *Pygmalion*. *Pretty Woman* turned out to be the surprise hit of the year, launching the career of a new female star, Julia Roberts, and putting Richard Gere just where he needed to be, near the top of every studio executive's casting list. He was hot again.

At the age of forty, Richard Gere has made a comeback on the strength of *Pretty Woman*. In Hollywood, that's a male prerogative. Women seldom get a second chance. Today, Julia Roberts is the hottest female star in Hollywood, thanks to the same movie. She is twenty-two years old. She deserves at least as much credit as Gere does, perhaps more, for the success of *Pretty Woman*. But whatever Gere and Roberts do next, one thing is certain – her fee will be a fraction of his and it won't be because of his seniority. That concept doesn't exist in Hollywood. Moreover, if her career turns out to be as rocky as Gere's was, the chances of Julia Roberts making a comparable comeback at the age of forty are, quite frankly, nil. What Meryl Streep wryly refers to as the 'age police' will see to that. The disparity between their fees will have nothing to do with Roberts and Gere as individuals. It's just a fact that male stars are paid much more than female stars – usually twice or sometimes even three times as much – and their careers as stars tend to last far longer. Meryl Streep complained that when she co-starred with Jack Nicholson in

Ironweed, not only was Nicholson paid twice as much as she was, but when the movie flopped she, not Nicholson, attracted the bulk of the blame. 'There are different rules for women than there are for men,' says Streep.

'Women have identity problems as stars,' according to Anne Thompson, who writes a regular column on the movie business for *LA Weekly*. 'The audience doesn't know exactly who they are unless they really firm up a persona. Goldie Hawn had one – the dizzy blond. Goldie did very well in comedies like *Private Benjamin* and *Foul Play*. She's been trying to get her career back on track but she may be an example of a problem that women have, which is that they don't age as well as men. But how old can you be and play a dizzy blond?'

Goldie Hawn was a hit in Private Benjamin, *but how old can you be and still play a dizzy blonde?*

The studio bosses who decide what movies are made, who is in them and on what terms, maintain that the earnings disparity between male and female stars is market led. 'I suppose it has been subjectively proven over the years that most females do not sell tickets at the box office,' says Ned Tanen. 'Tom Cruise will open a movie. Eddie Murphy will open a movie. I can't think of one woman who will open a movie. It may get great reviews, it may be revered by the critics, but that does not mean that the public wishes to see them in the movie.' Even ex-Columbia Pictures president, Dawn Steel, has to admit there is a problem. 'I have to say that as a woman running a studio, I was very conscious of trying to make movies with women, but I also had in the back of my head the question, "At what level are these movies going to open?" The fact of the matter is, if you look at the movies starring women, they do not bring in as much money as movies starring certain men. If you go back and you look at all the women who have made movies over the last couple of years, I don't think you'll find one that opened to the level of an Eddie Murphy or a Schwarzenegger or a Stallone or a Mel Gibson.'

According to Joe Roth, the chairman of Twentieth Century Fox, 'Much of what sells big in the movie business are outsized, fantasy, action pictures and I think that men have a very difficult time going to see women in these roles. Male stars get paid more than female stars because men will go out to see men, and women will go out to see men, and men have a difficult time going out to see women. I think, frankly, it is sexism.' Of the top one hundred movies of all time it's no easy task finding a woman as the protagonist in the film. The highest grossing female buddy comedy movie is *Outrageous Fortune*, which grossed $57 million. That's like a mid-range male buddy comedy movie. Today, the only woman in the world who is an action star, who can actually carry a movie on her own from a box-office standpoint, is Sigourney Weaver. And it appears that even her credentials are suspect.

'I remember *Alien* being a kind of sleeper,' is how Dawn Steel recalls the science fiction horror movie that made Sigourney Weaver a star. 'I don't know that anybody expected it to do the business it did, and I don't know it did the business it did because of Sigourney. It was a horror genre in a way that had never been done before. Put Sigourney in something that's less a genre film then let's see.' Steel's doubts about Weaver's box-office clout are symptomatic of the attitude to female stars within the industry at large. There's a tendency to accept that the market leads the way, and the box-office failure of recent action movies starring female protagonists – *Blue Steel* with Jamie Lee Curtis and *Impulse* with Teresa Russell – are cited to support that argument. Furthermore, international pre-sales, which are inflating the earnings of male stars, do not work in the same way when women are brought into the equation. An informal poll by the *Hollywood Reporter* found that even for actresses of the calibre of Meryl Streep and Sigourney Weaver, 'pre-sales depend on the quality of the director or one other element brought to the package,' in other words, a male co-star. 'The way films are financed is in part to blame,' says Meryl Streep, referring to the dominance in foreign markets of action-adventure movies with male stars. 'You don't have to know the language to know something is exploding and to enjoy that spectacle. So what we're watching at home is dictated by tastes in the Far East and South-east Asia.'

But Hollywood's readiness to absolve itself of responsibility by blaming the audience is a self-fulfilling prophecy. Because producers and executives assume movies with a female lead will not make money, they don't try making them. And because writers know that it's difficult, if not impossible, to sell those kind of stories to producers and executives, they don't bother to write them. Hollywood used to make the same kind of assumptions about black movies until Spike Lee and Robert Townsend showed that a substantial audience for those movies existed. And, years back, stars like Bette Davis opened and carried movies without the buttress of a male star. 'Female actresses, I believe, are definitely underpaid,' says Ed Limato, the agent who represents Michelle Pfeiffer as well as Richard Gere and Mel Gibson. 'I don't believe female stars are given the opportunities that they should be given. I think that goes along with the lack of risk-taking in the industry.'

But power to change the way the business works comes to those with the commercial muscle to effect those changes. The rates of pay for female stars will improve only if that serves the commercial interests of the studios. In Hollywood, money talks. As Streep says, 'There's profit in the old way of doing things. It's the bottom line that drives the dream machine.' Director, Sydney Pollack, who has worked with some of the biggest female stars in the business – Barbra Streisand, Jane Fonda, Sally Field, Meryl Streep – admits that the film industry is totally driven by economics. 'Anything that works economically will happen in this business. I don't care what it is. If the economics of the business say that a female star will generate on her own a $200 million hit, you'll watch how fast that female star will get paid exactly what the male will get. The bottom line is money. If a woman will make them as much money as a man, believe me, they'll pay the woman.'

If any one individual can be credited with founding the star system, then Carl Laemmle deserves that dubious honour. In 1910, Laemmle, a struggling producer, poached from the American Biograph Company a popular young actress called Florence Lawrence, who was known to her many fans merely as The Biograph Girl. The first moguls, rightly suspecting the power of those forces they were in danger of unleashing against themselves, had made a forlorn attempt to brand-name their movie stars with corporate labels and thus strangle any potential star system at birth. When movies began they had been spectacles in themselves. The mere phenomenon of moving images was sufficient to lure the public into paying for the privilege of sitting in a dark room with their eyes open wide. But that novelty soon wore thin. Something else was needed. Stories came first. And then the stars. The men who ran these early production companies feared, with good reason as it turned out, that their leading players would demand higher fees once they secured public recognition. As a consequence, the earliest stars were anonymous by design. Their names were deliberately concealed from the moviegoing public. Instead they were known by their company affiliation – 'The Biograph Girl' or 'The Vitagraph Girl'. But the attempt to brand-name the movies in this way was short-lived, thanks to Carl Laemmle.

Shortly after signing Miss Lawrence, for a much higher fee than Biograph was then paying her, Laemmle spread the story that she was dead. But as soon as the story of Miss Lawrence's demise had hit the headlines, Laemmle mounted a lavish advertising campaign accusing his competitors of maliciously circulating the lie to discredit his new star. He promised that Miss Lawrence would appear in person in St Louis on the day that her new movie opened in that city. Laemmle's aggressive publicity campaign had the desired effect. The arrival of Florence Lawrence at the St Louis railway station attracted an enormous crowd and on her return to New York more people flocked to greet her than had turned out to see the President of the United States a few weeks before. Carl Laemmle went on to found Universal Studios. As for Florence Lawrence, she finished her career as an extra for MGM and committed suicide in 1938.

The metamorphosis of the Biograph Girl into Florence Lawrence marked the birth of the movie star. Laemmle's competitors reluctantly followed his example and, as they had feared all along, star salaries shot up. In 1917 Douglas Fairbanks earned $780 000, making

Douglas Fairbanks, in a characteristically swashbuckling part for The Black Pirate, *was, by 1917, the highest paid movie star in the world.*

him the highest paid movie star of his time. Two years later the comedian Fatty Arbuckle was pulling in $1 million a year. And it wasn't long before Mary Pickford and Charlie Chaplin were earning much more than that. Fairbanks and Arbuckle and Chaplin and Pickford knew full well that they were the reason people came to

Charlie Chaplin and Mary Pickford knew that their names alone filled the theatres with moviegoers, and in 1919 they founded United Artists, with Douglas Fairbanks.

see their films and that their names meant more than the title of the movies they were in. Arbuckle's career was destroyed by a much-publicized scandal, but in 1919 Fairbanks, Chaplin and Pickford went on to found United Artists in an attempt to control their careers and exploit their popularity. Their initiative gave rise to the famous comment – 'The lunatics have taken over the asylum' – but their example did not set a trend. Most stars opted to stay inside the asylum, although in time they learned to loosen the straps of their strait-jackets.

During the next thirty years the studio bosses perfected the Hollywood star system. Louis B. Mayer, Sam Goldwyn and their fellow moguls would regularly travel to Europe to discover fresh new faces and launch them in America. Signed to long-term contracts, the embryonic stars would be nurtured through a rigorous course of classes covering elocution, acting, dancing and singing. Their faces would be powdered and plucked to conform to the tastes of the day. Lit by some of the world's finest portrait photographers, their lips and eyes and hair would be glossed and painted and permed to perfection. New lives and new names would be invented as the studio publicity department rejigged the young star's biography to cater to the demands of the gossip columnists. The studios owned these contract players, and their professional lives, sometimes their personal lives as well, were defined according to the judgement of the studio bosses.

Among all the men who ran the studios during the years when the contract system still prevailed, none was a more consummate creator of stars than David O. Selznick, the maverick producer of *A Star is Born*, *Gone With the Wind* and *Rebecca*. Selznick can be credited with launching the careers of Ingrid Bergman, Joan Fontaine, Jennifer Jones and Vivien Leigh. He is famous for the memos he sent to everyone with whom he worked, full as they are of detailed suggestions on how the careers of his stars should be nurtured and exploited. In 1936, he wrote to Richard Boleslawski, the director of *The Garden of Allah*, advising him to pay more attention to Marlene Dietrich's hair. 'Would you *please* speak to Marlene about the fact that her hair is getting so much attention and is being coiffed to such a degree that all reality is lost.' Three years later, he was preoccupied with renaming his fledgling star, Phyllis Walker. 'Where the hell is that new name for Phyllis Walker? ... Personally, I would like to decide on Jennifer and get a one-syllable last name that has some rhythm to it and that is easy to remember.' Jennifer Jones was the result. Selznick took more care than any other executive in Hollywood when it came to casting his contract players in roles that would show their best qualities. But even so, as the years wore on he found that his protégés became more defiant. When Joan Fontaine refused to accept a role Selznick wanted her to play he fired off a furious memo which expresses the sentiment of every studio executive before or since: 'I must say that I have known few film actors, even those with vast experience, who have had sound judgement about what they should do.'

Even while they were under contract to the studio, some of the biggest stars sought to flex their muscles by defying their bosses. During the thirties, James Cagney, who was contracted to Warner Brothers at $4500 a week, was one of Hollywood's biggest stars. But Cagney grew tired of being cast in the gangster movies which had made him famous. He wanted to try his hand at serious dramatic roles. In 1936 he successfully sued the studio and released himself from the contract. Two years later Cagney was back at Warners with a new three-year contract which guaranteed him $150 000 per picture, plus a cut of the profits. Bette Davis was another disgruntled star who fought Warners over many years. By 1943, she had her own company and a hefty 35 per cent share of the net profits on the movies she made for the studio. By the end of that decade the

Hollywood studios were buckling under the onslaught of federal regulation and the growth of television. The contract system collapsed and the stars, aided and abetted by their agents, learned how to cut the kind of deals that made the lavish weekly fees the studios had routinely doled out over the years look like small change. The era of the superstar had dawned in Hollywood.

'It is indefinable what makes any star,' says Universal Pictures chief, Tom Pollock. 'If we knew that, we could bottle it and sell it and make lots of money out of it. It's just something that goes on between an actor and his audience through a camera and onto a film. I don't know what it is, but I know it when it's there, and it's there with Arnold.' The Arnold in question is Arnold Schwarzenegger, the Austrian-born bodybuilder who now ranks as one of the biggest box-office stars in the world. He may also be the quintessential movie star of his time – a walking, talking brand-name. Schwarzenegger is an entertainment business phenomenon. He, more than any other single star, personifies Hollywood's orientation towards a global market with action-adventures and quick-hit comedies sold on the strength of a star name. Although he was born outside the United States, Schwarzenegger has become as integral to his adopted country's popular culture as McDonalds. Around the world, his name alone sells movies. And Schwarzenegger exploits that asset with the same dedication that the fast food chain devotes to the international exploitation of ground meat. Indeed, at times Schwarzenegger talks about his own career as if he were a brand-name product. 'I know one thing. I have been very fortunate that every year the public's interest in me and in my films has gone up, whatever is on the market. If it is magazine covers, they sell better this year than last year, and last year they sold better than the year before, so there is increase all the time. When you look at the last five years there has been a steady increase. We hope it will continue like that.'

'He won't do a film just because he thinks it's going to be successful if it's a role he doesn't want to play,' explains Caan's agent, Guy McElwaine.

Compare a star like Schwarzenegger to a fallen actor-star like James Caan. When his portrayal of Sonny Corleone in Francis Ford Coppola's *The Godfather* earned him an Academy Award nomination, Caan became an instant star. 'All of a sudden,' says Caan, 'you become Jesus.' And then he blew it. In the wake of that success he was offered and turned down a string of star roles. When Caan rejected the lead in *One Flew Over the Cuckoo's Nest*, it went instead to Jack Nicholson. As Caan says now, 'I felt it was a wonderfully written thing but it wasn't visual. I didn't know Milos [Forman] was going to do such a great job as he did.' *One Flew Over the Cuckoo's*

Nest was the second highest grossing movie of 1975 and won five Academy Awards including Best Actor for Nicholson. Caan also turned down the role of the husband in *Kramer vs Kramer*, which went instead to Dustin Hoffman. The movie, which Caan dismissed as 'middle class horse shit', went on to be the biggest box-office earner of 1979 and won five Academy Awards, including Best Actor for Hoffman. Instead, Caan made a string of flops before dropping out of sight. Eight years later he resurfaced in Bob Reiner's *Misery*, a psychological thriller which was well-received as a return to form by an actor whose name is virtually unknown to the new generation of moviegoers. Today Caan is philosophical about his capsized career. 'If I say, "This is terrible and I won't do it", go to the bank, it'll make a fortune. And anything I like goes the other way.'

'He won't do a film just because he thinks it's going to be successful if it's a role he doesn't want to play,' explains Caan's agent, Guy McElwaine. 'He just won't do it. Sometimes we'll argue about that. This business is about commerce. It is a business. And if we don't make money then we won't have a business any more. It's not hard. It's simple economics.'

No one has to tell Arnold Schwarzenegger about the commercial imperatives of the movie business. It's second nature to him. Schwarzenegger has made a string of liabilities – his name, his bulk, his accent – work for him. With each movie he makes, he widens his audience appeal without ever over-extending himself. And, better than anyone else, he knows how to sell movies, which is by selling himself. James Caan pays his publicist to keep him out of the papers. Not Schwarzenegger: 'I realized very early on in my career that the most important thing is to publicize yourself; to be available for interviews; to get on the covers of magazines; to travel all over the world and hit the foreign Press; to systematically work your way up there so that people get to know you and become fans because that, in turn, will make them see your films.'

Schwarzenegger is one of the few major stars who will pull out the stops to promote his films in foreign markets. According to producer Albert S. Ruddy, that might account for as much as 50 per cent of a film's gross. Self-promotion comes naturally to Schwarzenegger. Other stars, like Caan, may shun the media but, when it suits him, Schwarzenegger works the press like a maestro. He devotes as much effort and skill to promoting his movies as he does to the making of them. His public persona, manufactured and refashioned over the last decade, is his greatest achievement, greater than the dozen or so championship bodybuilding trophies he has won, and greater than the millions of dollars he has made through his real-estate investments and his movies. 'I really only had a plan,' he says, 'when it came to creating and publicizing myself.'

A refugee from what he remembers as the small-minded, negative thinking, can't-do ethos of Austria, Schwarzenegger's second life in America has been an uninterrupted series of home runs. Although he lost the Mr Universe contest in 1968, his first foray on American soil, that was to be Schwarzenegger's sole defeat for seven years. Between 1969 and 1975 he was the undefeated bodybuilding champion of the world, winning the Mr Universe title five times, the Mr Olympia title seven times. The style of his stardom was fashioned during those years. He promoted himself, and the sport he had come to dominate, with equal vigour. Before Schwarzenegger arrived on the scene, the American press had shunned bodybuilding as an unsavoury hobby for freaks. Schwarzenegger changed all that. As soon as he had powered his way to the top he combined his natural commercial instincts with a ready charm to transform what had once been dismissed as a seedy side-bar event into big business. 'I never saw bodybuilding as an end as others do. I felt I had business potential, because I always had good instincts to buy and sell.' In the process he propelled himself from being the anonymous champion of a ghetto sport into a national celebrity.

But Schwarzenegger became bored with his unremitting success as the world's number one muscleman. He retired, a rich man infused with a renewed sense of purpose – to be a movie star – which, by his own account, had been his intention all along. Schwarzenegger set out to become a star with the same remorseless dedication that had propelled him to the top of the bodybuilding league. 'He had a very specific idea of what he wanted to do with his life,' says his agent, Louis Pitt. 'He had very clear goals. He wanted to be Number One.' At the beginning Schwarzenegger met tremendous resistance, but just as he had triumphed over failure as a bodybuilder when he first arrived in America, he strove to surpass his ignominious efforts as an actor. For his first movie – *Hercules Goes to New York* – his accent was so strong that his voice had to be dubbed. From there, the only place to go was up. Schwarzenegger decided that if he was going 'to get serious with the acting', he would have to apply himself with the same single-minded dedication he had devoted to bulking up his body. As a bodybuilder, he had trained for five hours a day to achieve his goal of being Number One. Schwarzenegger had invested the same kind of energy in the refashioning of his own body, as a corporate executive might devote to the development of a new line in consumer products. Now that he wanted to expand his market share of moviegoers, it seemed natural that he should follow the same strategy. 'I said, why shouldn't I put the same amount of time into acting? I went to a lot of acting classes, voice classes, accent removal classes and on and on and on. I mean I covered myself really well.'

Schwarzenegger's dedication paid dividends. The simultaneous release of *Stay Hungry* and the feature-length documentary, *Pumping Iron*, established him as more than just a hunk of meat. Schwarzenegger played the bodybuilder in both movies, but at least he could talk. And, as they say in Hollywood, the camera loved him. 'I think that there was scepticism on other people's part only because nobody had really succeeded in that area,' says Pitt. 'A number of performers had played Hercules and those kind of muscle characters but never got past that. Arnold's vision was beyond doing that. Looking at *Stay Hungry*, you could see that there was more to the person than bodybuilding, even though it was centred around that idea. Arnold wanted to be exploited, take that attention, take that notoriety, use that to beget other things. So it became a kind of systematic plot plan.'

From that point on, the graph of Schwarzenegger's career followed the smooth, upward trajectory of a perfectly marketed brand-name product. His international box-office appeal was first demonstrated in the two *Conan* movies. After the success of those sword-and-sorcery epics, he played a robotic assassin, the anonymous cyborg in James Cameron's science-fiction thriller, *The Terminator*. The movie, a smash success, made the names of everyone who was associated with it. But more than anyone else, the movie belonged to Schwarzenegger. The accent, the name, the body all worked for him and, as he does so well in real life, he managed to send himself up without undermining the character he was playing. In *The Terminator*, Schwarzenegger delivered the few lines he had to say with the dead-pan finesse of his boyhood hero, Clint Eastwood. He's been emulating Eastwood's example ever since.

As Schwarzenegger says himself, 'You have to have good idols, people that you admire, people that you want to be when you have finished with the whole thing. Clint Eastwood was the man who represented a lot of those qualities.' Schwarzenegger's admiration of Eastwood, which dated from his childhood in Austria, only grew when he came to California. 'I read a lot of his interviews and he

Conan the Republican: George Bush rewarded Schwarzenegger for his political support by appointing him chairman of the President's Council on Physical Fitness.

always represented a man of real substance. I realized how multi-talented he is, how he can produce films, how he can star in them, how he can direct films. I always felt that was someone I could keep as a role model and mould myself after. I always kept him in front as a vision, as something to shoot towards.' At the height of his popularity, Clint Eastwood was the world's number one box-office star, acceptable to audiences in both action movies – westerns and thrillers – and in comedies like *Every Which Way But Loose*, in which he co-starred with a chimp. In a similar way, Schwarzenegger has consolidated his position as an action-adventure star – in movies like

Predator, Commando and *Raw Deal* – before branching out into new areas. 'I always felt it was best,' he says, 'to build up a stock with an audience out there that will always go to see your movies. If you want to keep those people loyal, you have to provide them with what they enjoy seeing. But that doesn't mean you can't add on every time ten per cent of new stuff and gradually make them see a new side of you.'

Schwarzenegger's ability to diversify, to expand his franchise without alienating his core fans, is what distinguishes him from his arch-rival Sylvester Stallone. Stallone was a star well before Schwarzenegger, but for the last few years Stallone has found himself trapped within a cage of his own making. Audiences still flock to see him as *Rocky* or *Rambo* but his forays into new fields – be they romantic comedies like *Rhinestone*, or serious dramas like *FIST*, or even action-thrillers like *Cobra* – have been disastrous. And as the appeal of successive *Rockys* and *Rambos* inevitably fades, the cage only gets smaller. Sylvester Stallone is in trouble because, unlike Schwarzenegger, he has never learned how to spice his action-adventure movies with self-mockery. Audiences either take him as seriously as he takes himself or they laugh *at* him, not, for all that he might wish it, *with* him.

'Schwarzenegger is much, much smarter than almost any actor I've known,' says Ned Tanen. 'Schwarzenegger took what he is and he capitalized on it. Schwarzenegger found out a long time ago that he had a very specific image and that the only way he was going to capitalize on that image was to have fun with it and allow the audience to have some fun with it. He became a star because the public became a partner with him in what he was doing.' The apotheosis of that partnership was the comedy, *Twins*. Schwarzenegger and his agent, Louis Pitt, planned the movie with the same calculation as the people at Coke might devote to the launch of a new low-sugar thirst-quencher. Before *Twins*, Schwarzenegger's audience was primarily made up of kids and men up to the age of forty. 'Though he had a very strong female audience,' says Pitt, 'it had reached a certain level and then just levelled off. He kept getting repeat business. So we talked about how to figure out a way to include everybody.'

With the help of director Ivan Reitman and co-star, Danny DeVito, Schwarzenegger's comedy début turned out to be the most successful movie of his career. As Pitt explains, '*Twins* made Arnold accessible to everybody, to women, to men, to children, to people of all ages all over the world. Normally our comedies don't necessarily do that well foreign. This was a comedy that did exceptionally well.' *Twins* was the perfect high-concept comedy. The poster said it all: it depicted the hulking Schwarzenegger and the stubby DeVito dressed identically, grinning, standing beneath the one-word title and the copy-line, 'Only their mother could tell them apart'. It was a self-selling movie.

'Now,' says Schwarzenegger, 'my plan is to do action films and comedies and switch on and off, back and forth to show both sides.' Two brand-name product lines for the price of one. During the summer of 1990, he put the plan into effect. Over four months, Schwarzenegger devoted his considerable energies to the marketing of his latest movie, *Total Recall*. He began filming a new Ivan Reitman comedy, *Kindergarten Cop*, and he prepared himself to reprise his most famous role in the sequel to *The Terminator*. Schwarzenegger was not merely the star of *Total Recall*, a $60 million science-fiction extravaganza. He had also had a say in the buying of the script. He chose Paul Verhoeven, who had made his name in America as the director of the futuristic blockbuster, *Robocop*, to direct it. And with a 15 per cent share of *Total Recall*'s gross box-office takings, he had a personal interest in its success. Always serious about selling himself, Schwarzenegger approached the promotion of *Total Recall* as if it were a political campaign designed to capture the hearts and minds of the nation.

Vanity Fair. GQ. Smart. Premiere. Muscle & Fitness. Entertainment Weekly. TV Guide. During the summer months of 1990, the covers of all seven magazines featured the face of Arnold Schwarzenegger sporting a variety of expressions, well, two actually: expression number one was sharp and grim; expression number two was puppy-dog happy. Of course within those categories there were variants. Schwarzenegger was pictured grinning with his horse for *Vanity Fair*, grinning with a television set hoisted aloft for *TV Guide*, grinning underwater for *Premiere*. But the uniformity of the seven magazine covers far outweighed the minor differences between them, and this uniformity extended to the cover stories inside. The main event was Arnold Schwarzenegger: the success story; the consummate self-made man; a living, breathing personification of the American Dream. 'He has risen from a penniless 20-year-old immigrant to a 42-year-old movie star whose films grossed more than $1 billion during the 1980s,' reported *GQ* with a brand of breathless excitement that was characteristic of almost all the other profiles. 'Arnold's is the kind of success story that can make a man a true believer in the American way...'

In fact, Arnold's is the kind of success story that can make you a true believer in the malleability of the Press. Working the Press comes naturally to Schwarzenegger. His approach to interviews is faultless. During the first few seconds he will fix his interviewer with an intense look of fearsome concentration. The look is unnerving. It implies that any question which might ruffle Schwarzenegger's serenity will be rewarded with unspeakable retribution. In fact, the look is indicative of something else entirely. Schwarzenegger is listening. He is straining to figure out what the angle is. He already knows exactly what he wants to say. What he's trying to find out in those first few seconds is just how he should pitch the message so as to appeal most directly to the market he is trying to reach and to give the Press just what they need. He can talk about bodybuilding or babies, machine-guns or marriage, pumping iron or politics. And he can package anything he wants to say in nice, tasty anecdotes that are guaranteed to make it to the printed page, just as long as he can figure out the angle first. And in the three months leading up to the launch of *Total Recall*, Schwarzenegger was giving the Press just what they needed by the spadeful.

The first wave of exposure broke on the night of the Academy Awards. Arnold Schwarzenegger and Warren Beatty appeared as the guests of Barbara Walters on a TV show business special. The contrast between the two stars was illuminating. Beatty, who was an international star before Schwarzenegger could even speak English, is known for deploring the brand of publicity hype which has become the accepted means of launching a new movie and at which Schwarzenegger excels. The way Beatty sees it, the promotional circus detracts attention from the only thing that really matters, the movie itself. Beatty has led a reclusive existence, rarely speaking out and then only to lambast the Press for the inaccuracy of its reporting. He is especially critical of the way in which reviewers and journalists draw attention to the facts behind the making of the movie – its cost, the fees paid to the stars – which he feels are extraneous to the quality of the finished work. But the suspicion that his previous two movies – *Reds* and *Ishtar* – had suffered as a result of 'negative publicity' which he had done nothing to counter, persuaded him to exert himself now on behalf of his latest movie, *Dick Tracy*.

Dick Tracy was to be the Walt Disney Company's summer blockbuster. It was intended as their answer to one of the most hyped movies of all time, Warner's *Batman*, which had led the pack of the 1989 summer releases. In order to claim that movie's mantle, *Dick Tracy* would have to out-perform another potential summer blockbuster, *Total Recall*. The leading men of both movies appeared in separate interviews with Barbara Walters, aired at prime time on the network. The different ways in which Beatty and Schwarzenegger comported themselves that evening aptly illustrates their respective attitudes to the nature and the obligations inherent in movie stardom.

Beatty's performance on the Barbara Walters' show was lacklustre. The exchange between interviewer and interviewee rapidly settled into the adversarial mode that has become the trademark of Beatty's relationship with the Press. By contrast, Schwarzenegger's performance was superlative. Whereas Beatty's reluctance to be on the show was clear from the start, Schwarzenegger took charge with the disarming glee of a man in his *métier*. Beatty wanted to restrict the discussion to his work – and especially to the movie he was on the show to promote. When he was asked questions that touched on his personal life he bristled and turned coy. Schwarzenegger's life was an open book. He talked about his marriage to Maria Shriver, the newscaster and niece of John Kennedy. He joked about the gentle rivalry between his mother and his mother-in-law – one claiming that his new born daughter, Katherine Eunice, was more Schwarzenegger than Kennedy, the other that she was more Kennedy than Schwarzenegger. He talked about his charity work as the newly named chairman of the President's Council on Physical Fitness. Barbara Walters was visibly charmed and the message Schwarzenegger broadcast to the nation, via the pliant good services of his hostess, was to be echoed in almost every article about him that would appear in the Press over the next three months. That night, Arnold Schwarzenegger was stardom made wholesome.

The promotional campaign for *Total Recall* culminated in a lavish 'press junket'. The distributors of the movie invited fifty or so newspaper journalists from all over America and about half as many television and radio reporters to an exclusive preview of the movie, after which they all spent the night at a luxury hotel. The next morning the Press and radio reporters had breakfast with Schwarzenegger, his three co-stars, the director and the producer. Each table, accommodating eight journalists, would have the benefit of Schwarzenegger's undivided attention for ten minutes before a publicist moved him on to the adjoining table and his seat was filled by the director, Paul Verhoeven, or one of the cast. During the afternoon, the process was repeated for the television cameras. An interviewer would spend ten minutes with one of the six celebrities before moving on to the next stop. Immediately one reporter vacated his or her seat, another would step forward to occupy it. Schwarzenegger's attitude to the dozens of journalists who faithfully transcribed his every word is to the point. 'I mean this guy is only there for one thing and that is to sell your tickets, right? You say to the guy right away when he sits down, or the woman, I say, "We talk about the movie. That's it. Don't ask anything else, just the movie." And then you do a hundred interviews a day like that, just three minutes each. It might go to four minutes.' It was a gruelling process for most of the interviewees. Schwarzenegger revelled in it. And it paid off. *Total Recall* went on to gross over $120 million in the United States alone.

This is what makes Schwarzenegger the quintessential star of his time. He epitomizes the skill with which Hollywood manipulates the media. Of course, Hollywood and the Press have always enjoyed a relationship of incestuous collusion. During the heyday of studio power, the publicity departments of the majors operated as a virtual wire agency, sending out stories about the stars of the day, which were often printed word-for-word by a passive Press. Today, things are not so very different. Studios need publicity for movies, for which they would as soon as not have to pay. And magazine editors know very well that stars sell covers. This has meant that the Press, which is supposed to have some critical function, some adversarial function, has become merely another arm of the Hollywood publicity machine.

Hollywood's hold on the Press is so strong today because the media's demand for stars has reached fever pitch thanks to the arrival of dozens of new entertainment magazines and a host of new entertainment shows on television. According to *Variety*: 'The Hollywood publicist who used to have only four or five possible national outlets now has fifteen or twenty – and all of them are vying for exclusive interviews with the same people.' Kim Masters, who used to be contributing editor to the movie magazine *Premiere* before moving on to join the *Washington Post*, says, 'At this point, publicists in Hollywood have the power of somebody selling water in the desert. They're selling something people really need, which is stars. So publicists are able to set the terms for journalists.'

Journalists who write negative copy can be penalized. If a reporter displeases a star, that star will no longer be available and the reporter can be hurt. Kim Masters says she has been blacklisted by studios for writing things that displeased them. 'Nobody said that they were inaccurate or unfair. They just didn't like it in the newspaper.' But some journalists are to blame as much as the publicists. The Press tends to idolize the movies and a lot of star-struck reporters want to work for the studios. So there's a lot of timidity among the Press in Hollywood. They don't ask difficult questions because they don't want to make anybody mad. It's a very delicate relationship that leads to a lot of very insubstantial reporting. All this suits Hollywood just fine. A star-struck Press helps stars to sell movies. Were he alive, Carl Laemmle would be delighted.

CHAPTER FOUR

SCHMUCKS WITH APPLES

Working as a screenwriter, I always thought that 'Film is a collaborative business' only constituted half of the actual phrase. From a screenwriter's point of view, the correct rendering should be, 'Film is a collaborative business: bend over.'

David Mamet, screenwriter

They ruin your stories. They trample on your pride. They massacre your ideas. And what do you get for it? A fortune.

Anonymous writer

Here's a conundrum. It's a golden rule in Hollywood that you cannot make a movie without a script. A good screenplay is essential to the making of a successful movie. In fact, it is the one absolute indispensable. If the script stinks, nothing will save the movie from being a dud. 'It is totally impossible to make a great picture out of a lousy script,' says the veteran filmmaker, Billy Wilder, who adds, 'It is impossible, on the other hand, for a mediocre director to screw up a great script altogether.' And yet, despite Wilder's veneration for the screenplay, it is somehow appropriate that in *Sunset Boulevard*, Wilder's classic satire on Hollywood, the narrator, a screenwriter played by William Holden, should end up dead. There he is, floating face down in a swimming-pool, the ultimate

The fall guy: in Sunset Boulevard, *William Holden's screenwriter falls foul of Gloria Swanson's star and meets his end in a way entirely appropriate to Los Angeles.*

patsy. That's the conundrum: if good screenplays are so sought after, why is it that writers are treated like third-class citizens in Hollywood?

The writer of an original screenplay – that's a screenplay resulting from an original idea rather than taken from a book or from some other source – is like a virgin in Babylon. No one is more desired than a writer with a hot property, a commercial script which every studio and producer in town wants to buy. 'I don't know of anything that generates the excitement of the chase after a big script,' says John Goldwyn, who was until recently a senior production executive at MGM/UA Communications. After weeks, months, maybe years, of solitary confinement, a writer may find to his surprise that every young blood in town is lusting for him. A host of eager suitors are competing for his favour and they're prepared to pay generously. 'Some writers are now making more money than they ever dreamed,' says Phil Alden Robinson, who wrote *Rhinestone* and *Field of Dreams*. 'A couple of years ago, $200 000 was a great price for a script. Now, it's not uncommon to hear of writers getting $500 000 for a rewrite, or $800 000 for an original screenplay. Just a couple of years ago, those numbers were unheard of.'

In the first few months of 1990 alone, a clutch of screenplays by relatively inexperienced writers sold for upwards of $1 million each and the latest script by *Lethal Weapon* writer, Shane Black, went to Warners for a then record breaking $1.75 million. Then along came Joe Eszterhas with an original screenplay called *Basic Instinct*. Eszterhas, who wrote the screenplays for *Flashdance*, *Jagged Edge* and *Music Box*, sold *Basic Instinct* for $3 million to Carolco. Though only a handful enjoy such rewards, it's not surprising that writers of highly desirable original screenplays may feel a brief, joyful rush of power. It should be savoured, because that sweet moment lasts only as long as the writer retains his or her virginity. Once a deal is made and they surrender their precious treasure, they will find that their allure has evaporated. Now that they have been deflowered, nobody wants to know them. The fact that Joe Eszterhas received $3 million for *Basic Instinct* did nothing to protect him from the whim of the people who bought the script. He was off the project less than two months after the sale. As ever, creative differences were cited as the reason. 'You sit at home,' says Phil Alden Robinson. 'You write a screenplay. You give it to a studio and they say, "Thank you. Here's your money. Go away."'

The economics of the movie business do not work to the writer's advantage. As Academy Award-nominated screenwriter, Roger Simon says, 'The writer is perfectly placed to be dumped on'. For one thing, they come along early in the production process when relatively little money is at stake. It's easy to fire writers because they are expendable, in the dealmaker's jargon, they have no leverage. 'The clout you have depends entirely on how *useful* you are to the people as the picture moves through the various stages,' says William Goldman, who wrote the screenplays for *Butch Cassidy and the Sundance*

Kid, *Marathon Man*, and *All the President's Men*. And the writer's usefulness normally expires on delivery of the screenplay.

Once the movie goes into production, the writer is entirely at the mercy of the director and the star, especially the star because, once the cameras are turning, the star can effectively hold the movie to ransom. 'When the film is being made,' says Phil Alden Robinson, 'and the meter is running and the money is being spent every second, a studio executive is going to say to himself, "You know what? The star can cost me a lot of money if he's unhappy right now. So I'm going to make him happy."' Robinson found to his cost what it takes to make a star happy when he sold a story called *Rhinestone* to Twentieth Century Fox. The studio cast major stars – Dolly Parton and Sylvester Stallone – in the modest story Robinson had crafted. And then, Robinson says, to make Stallone happy, Fox allowed him to rewrite virtually every word of the script. Why did the studio let their star transform a story with which they were already satisfied? Because conventional wisdom has it that the star's name on the

Phil Alden Robinson's screenplay for Rhinestone, *which starred Sylvester Stallone and Dolly Parton, was drastically changed to appease Stallone.*

cinema marquee guarantees a strong opening weekend at the box office. The writer is in no position to argue. *His* name in neon won't even bring in small change. 'Nobody goes to the movies because Roger Simon wrote it or even Robert Towne wrote it,' says Simon. In the case of *Rhinestone*, the studio was wrong. The movie bombed.

Robinson admits that it is almost impossible for a writer to protect his or her work. 'They either hire another writer to come in and change it into something that you didn't intend it to be, or they hire a director or an actor who will change it into something that you didn't intend it to be. You have somehow to convince the director, or the star, or the studio executive, "I'm your guy. I'll make the changes you want to make but I'll make them so they don't violate the intention of the script." You don't always have a choice.' It is not unusual for a studio to buy a screenplay for the core idea and then proceed to hire a succession of writers to remodel it. Studio executives, stars, directors and producers, too, may all have a hand in reworking the script long after the original author has been dismissed. Unfortunately for professional screenwriters, almost everyone in Hollywood is under the illusion that they can write. Writing screenplays may seem to be easy but writing them well is about as difficult as anything you can imagine. Stars, studio executives and anyone else who fancies meddling with the script seem only to appreciate the first part of that little dictum. For real writers, it is understandably exasperating. 'You have people making hundreds of thousands of dollars a year and if something went wrong with their plumbing, they wouldn't get down on their knees with a bunch of wrenches,' says writer Howard Rodman, 'but if there is something wrong with a screenplay, they assume that they know how to fix it.'

But the screenwriter's right to retain exclusive control of his or her work is untenable because filmmaking is an intrinsically collaborative enterprise. A screenplay may be an essential first step towards making a movie, but it is only the first step. All writers are protective about their work, but while other kinds of writers – novelists, essayists, poets – can afford to be proprietory, screenwriters are in no position to be so tenacious. Nora Ephron has worked as a journalist, novelist and screenwriter. She wrote the scripts for *Silkwood*, *When Harry Met Sally*, and adapted her own autobiographical book into the screenplay for *Heartburn*, which starred Jack Nicholson and Meryl Streep. She spent her childhood in Los Angeles – her parents were screenwriters – but she has lived in New York by choice for many years now. She came to movie-writing fairly late in life, after she had already established herself as a successful writer in other fields. 'When you write an essay, when you write a book, maybe an editor says, "Do you want to change a little of this or a little of that?" But pretty much what you write is what the reader reads. This is so far from the truth in movies that it's absolutely staggering, and it takes you quite a long time to accommodate yourself to that and to get used to it.'

No matter what its intrinsic merit, a screenplay has no cultural significance until it is brought to life on the screen. Writers have to accommodate themselves to the fact that though screenplays are, in the words of writer-director Paul Schrader, 'invitations to others to collaborate on a work of art, they are not in themselves works of art.' The existence of characters, the situations in which they find themselves, the way they behave, the words they say, have to exist on paper but that existence is transient. According to Schrader, 'the only reason that it needs to be written down is so that it can be remembered, memorized, rewritten, sold ...' Herschel Weingrod, who wrote the screenplay for *Trading Places*, likens the role of a writer to that of an architect. 'Basically, you're being asked to do the blueprints for a house that will be built by other people and lived in by still other people and, hopefully, it's going to come out in the manner that you intended ... if you're lucky.' The analogy is a little misleading because the people who build houses are not in the habit of changing the plans as they go along. Nora Ephron has a more apt metaphor. She likens writing a screenplay to making a pizza. At the beginning it is plain and simple, just as the writer likes. 'You give it to the director, and the director says, "I love this pizza, but don't you think it should have mushrooms on it?" So you put some mushrooms on. Then they cast the movie and they say, "Pepperoni! It really needs some pepperoni." Then the costume person comes in – "Anchovies" – and the next thing you know, you have a pizza with everything. Sometimes you taste it and you say, "Why did I let them put the pepperoni on? I knew it was wrong." And sometimes you are exultant that the collaboration worked so wonderfully and you have this delicious thing. On the other hand, there is no question that it is very, very rare that all this collaboration makes something better.'

All writers need to sell their work but whereas a novelist can get by with 15 000 or so readers, a screenwriter needs a larger base of support. 'If you have a good idea but you don't think it's going to appeal to several million people, then you shouldn't even waste your time writing it,' says Schrader. 'You have chosen the wrong medium.' Screenplays have to be sold many times over, to a financier or a studio, to a director and a cast of actors who must be persuaded to devote their time and energy to making the movie, to a distributor who will invest in the release and the marketing of the finished film, and finally to an audience of moviegoers. A screenplay may be the writer's *ultimate* statement, but it is only a first step towards the final movie. That will come many months, and many millions of dollars later. According to Howard Rodman, 'When you are writing a screenplay, one of the things you are doing, in a sense, is writing a prospectus for a stock offering.'

Commercial necessity is no excuse for the ways in which writers are sometimes brutally treated but much of the sympathy that often automatically accrues to screenwriters is misplaced. It sounds shocking that a writer might be fired or that the script might be rewritten by the director without the original writer's agreement, but movies often have to be made that way. What the writer writes, a director must direct, and no director who is of any worth can direct from a script which he or she does not instinctively feel is right. 'I feel, right or wrong, that I could read a script, love the idea and know very well from the script that that writer could not rewrite the script the way I would want it,' says Sydney Pollack. That is exactly what happened on Pollack's movie *Tootsie*. The original screenplay was about a male tennis player who tried to pass himself off as a female player. Several rewrites, and several writers later, it emerged as Dustin Hoffman struggling to get work as an actor by impersonating a woman.

Most writers accept being rewritten as a routine occupational hazard. That's not to say they always take it in their stride. 'When another writer is brought on to something you've written, you really feel lousy,' says Tom Schulman, who won an Academy Award for his original screenplay for *Dead Poets Society*. 'You feel like a failure. It's like getting fired from a job. You wonder whether your career is over. You worry every day about why it happened, did you blow it and all that. The feeling of being rewritten is a lousy feeling.' 'Written out' is the rather brutal term used to describe a writer who has outlived his or her usefulness and therefore has to be replaced. According to Lindsay Doran, who runs Sydney Pollack's production company, Mirage Enterprises, 'Feeling that a writer is written out is the most horrible thing that can possibly happen. I never try to start a process without thinking that I can finish with that person, that they can do the whole job.'

Doran's painstaking approach to nurturing screenplays is exceptional in Hollywood. Many executives, producers or directors adopt a different approach. They think nothing of working with several writers, either sequentially or, more rarely, simultaneously. Howard Rodman describes the two techniques as akin to serial monogamy and an orgy. It's not uncommon for an executive to say, 'We'll start with this writer because she can give us the structure, and then later on we'll bring somebody else in to do the characters.' This nuts and bolts approach to screenwriting – the script as an assembly-line product – is especially common to 'high-concept' movies where the storyline can be accurately condensed into a single short sentence. And like the automobile assembly line, it is always possible to streamline the process a stage further. When Disney wanted to develop a sequel to the enormously successful *Three Men and a Baby*, they hired three separate teams of writers to work simultaneously on what eventually became *Three Men and a Little Lady*.

Ivan Reitman, the director of such hit comedies as the *Ghostbusters* movies and *Twins*, is a keen practitioner of the nuts and bolts school of screenwriting. For *Kindergarten Cop*, a high-concept vehicle for Arnold Schwarzenegger, which casts him as a tough city cop who finds himself working undercover as a kindergarten teacher, Reitman began by fleshing out the script with the original writer, Murray Salem. 'Ivan was not that friendly to me,' recalls Salem. 'We would have a meeting. He would tell me, "I want this." And then he would get up and look out of the window. And I'm sitting there saying, "Well, I wonder if this meeting is over or not?"' After a couple of months Reitman felt Salem was 'written out' on the story. The screenplay had a strong concept but the premise had not been developed to its full potential. 'I felt we needed someone else's help,' he says. Reitman asked Salem if he minded him bringing in two new writers. 'It was a bit like Napoleon asking Luxembourg if he can invade,' recalls Salem, 'I mean, I had to say, "Yes".'

Reitman then brought in Tim Harris and Herschel Weingrod, the writers of the hit comedy, *Trading Places*. They had worked with Reitman before, most recently on the rewrite for *Twins*. Like many successful screenwriters, they work as a team. 'It's almost like being twins in the psychic sense that you finish each other's thoughts,' explains Harris. Reitman isolated those sections of the script he was unhappy about and Harris and Weingrod went to work. Rewrite work is tough but it has its compensations – it's very, very well paid and there's the gratification of knowing that you are writing to a specific purpose. 'I think you get burned out [by rewrite work],' says Harris, 'but it's exciting when you know that the words you're writing today are going to be picked up and they're going to be on Ivan's desk within an hour and they'll be incorporated into the script and they're actually going to be spoken.'

For the first draft, Reitman briefed Harris and Weingrod not to go for laughs – those would come later. The priority was to get the structure right. They produced two more drafts and Reitman still wasn't completely satisfied. Eight weeks before filming was due to start, the panic set in. 'We really needed more funny lines, more interesting situations, more twists,' says Reitman. 'So I asked that two other writing teams help them out as well.' Now there were three writing teams working on the screenplay at the same time. They all knew of each other's existence. They read each other's material. Every couple of days, Reitman would get ten pages from one, another fifteen pages from another, and he would go home and weave them together so that they made some intelligent sense as one script.

Babaloo Mandel and Lowell Ganz are one of the teams Reitman hired to polish the screenplay. Mandel and Ganz have written a clutch of original screenplays such as *Night Shift*, *Splash* and *Parenthood* for director Ron Howard. They also take rewrite work. 'Rewrites come under different headings,' says Mandel. 'One time a producer came to us and said, "We've got this wonderful, brilliant script, except we hate the lead character". So what we had to do was suck out the lead character and replace him without touching the body of the script.

Director Ivan Reitman, seen here on the set of Kindergarten Cop *with Arnold Schwarzenegger, used several writers to get the screenplay in shape.*

It's a little harder because we have to alter our style to fit seamlessly into the script. We try to make it so, when you are watching the film, it looks like one writer. We're basically tailors. You want the cuffs this short? Fine.'

Reitman cites historical precedent for the way he works with writers. 'This is the way that some of the great Hollywood movies in the forties and fifties were written. It was easier then because the studios had writers on contract. There was a big building full of writers and the Head of Production would come in and say, "OK guys, this goes in seven weeks. It's called *Casablanca*. It really needs some work". And about four teams would start to work on it simultaneously, each taking a different problem.' Then as now, the assignment of so many writers created problems when it came time to compile the final credits. Cases where more than one writer has worked on a screenplay are the norm rather than the exception in Hollywood and the accreditation of authorship can sometimes be acrimonious. In the old days of the contract system, before the Writer's Guild was set up to fight such practices, the screenwriting credit was at the behest of the producer. Now when a screenwriting credit is under dispute between several writers, the Writer's Guild must arbitrate between them. Every draft of the various screenplays, together with any notes or correspondence pertaining to the works, are read by three anonymous Guild members who then apportion the credit as they see fit. The system is far from perfect but it is an improvement on the bad old days when the exhausted contract writer might find, as the end titles rolled, that his hard-earned screenwriting credit had been given to the producer's son-in-law. Of course, sometimes the writer doesn't want the credit. On occasion, taking his or her name *off* the credits is the writer's final recourse. When a writer joins the Writer's Guild, he or she can register a pseudonym. According to Howard Rodman, 'to be able to yank your name from something when you don't like it is one of the great pleasures of being a screenwriter.'

If that is one of life's sweetest pleasures, then seeing your ideas attributed to some other writer without your knowledge or consent must be one of life's sharpest pains. As Dorothy Parker observed, 'The only -ism Hollywood believes in is plagiarism.' Although writers who suspect they have been plagiarized have recourse in law, plagiarism is difficult and expensive to prove and only a handful of cases come to trial. Of course, many allegations of plagiarism are merely nuisance suits to harass the makers of a recent blockbuster into paying off the litigant. If a case does have merit, the plagiarist will try to settle out of court.

January 1990 was a bonanza month when four plagiarism suits hit the headlines. Amy Heckerling, the writer-director of the 1989 hit movie, *Look Who's Talking*, found herself facing a $20-million suit and the allegation that she had taken the idea for her movie from a twenty-minute student film and other story materials which had been shown to her four years earlier. In the same month, George Lucas appeared in a Canadian court to defend himself in a $129-million copyright infringement case. A Canadian writer-producer, Dean Preston, alleged that the Ewoks, the cute, furry, and rather irritating teddy bear-like creatures who featured in Lucas' *Return of the Jedi*, were his own invention. Preston alleged the Ewoks made their début in his screenplay, *Space Pets*, which he said he had mailed to Lucas five years before the movie's release. Also in January 1990, Christopher Reeve found himself as a co-defendant in a case where two writers alleged they had sent him an unsolicited treatment which became the story basis for *Superman IV*.

Whatever the individual merits or lack of them represented by these cases, suits for plagiarism are a major headache that studios and producers are at pains to avoid. All studios and most producers seek to protect themselves by refusing to accept unsolicited material unless it comes through an agent. For their part, writers submitting material try to protect their property by registering it with the Writer's Guild. On balance, though, it is the writer who remains the most vulnerable.

A notable exception, which however only proves the rule, was the $5-million breach of contract case brought by Art Buchwald against Paramount Pictures. In March 1983, Art Buchwald, the humorist and Pulitzer Prize-winning newspaper columnist, made a deal with Paramount Pictures to develop two scripts from a story he had written called *King for a Day*. Paramount spent more than $400 000 in their attempt to produce an acceptable screenplay. Two and a half years later, when Paramount's management changed, the studio let the option lapse and Buchwald took his idea to Warner Brothers. But Warners eventually held off taking the idea any further when they heard that a similar story was about to go into production at Paramount. The movie was *Coming to America* starring Paramount's most valuable star, Eddie Murphy, and it eventually grossed between $300 and $400 million worldwide. In America, the movie was the third highest grosser of the year behind *Rain Man* and *Who Framed Roger Rabbit?* According to the credits, two writers, David Sheffield and Barry W. Blaustein, wrote the screenplay of *Coming to America* from an original story by Eddie Murphy. But according to Buchwald and his producer, Alain Bernheim, the plot of *Coming to America* had been lifted from the eight-page treatment Paramount Pictures had optioned from him five years earlier.

The case promised to be a show trial. Buchwald's lawyers said that it was their intention 'to send a message throughout the entertainment industry that powerful motion picture studios may not option the original works of writers, use the works, disregard with impunity their obligations to pay for them, and then brazenly deny their misconduct in an arrogant display of conspicuous bad faith.' Buchwald won his case which, by the time of its resolution, had become a *cause célèbre*. The court awarded him and Alain Bernheim $250 000 and a 19 per cent share of the net profits of *Coming to America*. Paramount subsequently claimed that the movie, despite having grossed over $350 000 million, was not yet in profit but Buchwald, who went back to court to challenge this, had won the moral victory. However, for every Buchwald, who has both the will and the means to contest an injury, there are countless writers who suffer their abuse in silence. The Buchwald case stands out as the exception.

The beleaguered screenwriter is one of the stock characters of motion picture mythology and his solitary battle against studio bosses, rapacious producers and directors with overblown egos – in a word, the philistines – is an ancient and familiar scenario. The Suffering Screenwriters made their inglorious début in the years when the studios ruled Hollywood and the contract system was the law of the land. Studio executives trawled the continent for the finest writers, lured them to Hollywood with the promise of limitless lucre and then, once the catch was safely hauled in, sucked out their souls. Writers were put under contract to the studio. They were owned by the studio. The studio could do with them as it wished. And most of the time, the writers, 'schmucks with Underwoods,' as Jack Warner dubbed them, did what they were told. Of course, no one *made* them write for the movies. They were slaves by choice. By contrast with the earnings they could garner from journalism or literature, the rewards for working in movieland were obscenely generous.

Many of the very best men and women of letters who were tempted to Hollywood came for the cash. Ben Hecht, a prolific Chicago newspaperman, was lured west by an irresistible telegram from his friend, Herman Mankiewicz, who co-authored *Citizen Kane* with Orson Welles: 'Will you accept three hundred per week to work for Paramount Pictures. All expenses paid. The three hundred is peanuts. Millions are to be grabbed out here and your only competition is idiots. Don't let this get around.'

Despite, or rather because of, the promise of unprecedented riches, the new recruits arrived in Hollywood laden with qualms about the movie business. They were rarely disappointed. No matter how murky their deepest suspicions were, the reality invariably proved to be much worse. The biggest fish documented their woes in ghoulish detail. Raymond Chandler, William Faulkner, Ben Hecht, F. Scott Fitzgerald and Dorothy Parker coined some of their most memorable *bons mots* while venting their spleen on the movie colony. Chandler's description of Los Angeles as 'a city with all the personality of a paper cup' – a description likely to dog it till the end of time – is, perhaps, a worthy rejoinder for his years of well-paid anguish.

Among the early generation of Hollywood scribes, no one was more keen to bite the hand that fed him than Ben Hecht. Not long after arriving in Hollywood, Hecht found he was being paid from $50 000 to $125 000 a script. 'Tremendous sums of money,' he said, for work 'that required no more effort than a game of pinochle.' *Scarface*, *The Front Page*, *Wuthering Heights*, *His Girl Friday* and *Notorious* were some of the film scripts he wrote, either alone or in collaboration with Charles MacArthur, not that Hecht took much pride in what he regarded as overpaid hackwork. And Hecht was paid even more for rewriting, uncredited, the work of others. For one week's work, salvaging the script for *Gone With the Wind*, Hecht received $15 000 from producer David O. Selznick. But, looking back twenty years later, Hecht claimed to have forgotten every one of the sixty scripts he penned in Hollywood, most of which, he said, took him less than a fortnight to write.

A champion cynic in a city of dreamers, Hecht was under no illusions why he was being paid such riches: 'I have always considered that half of the large sum paid me for writing a movie script was in payment for listening to the producer and obeying him. I am not being facetious. The movies pay as much for obedience as for creative work. An able writer is paid a larger sum than a man of small talent. But he is paid this added money not to use his superior talents.'

Ben Hecht was a born cynic who never forgave Hollywood for paying him a fortune to do work he despised.

Raymond Chandler, the novelist and screenwriter, dismissed Los Angeles as a city with all the personality of a paper cup.

Hecht may have started his screenwriting career with an air of jaunty cynicism but by the end he was profoundly appalled. 'The movies are one of the bad habits that corrupted our century,' he wrote in his memoirs, 'an eruption of trash that has lamed the American mind and retarded Americans from becoming a cultured people.'

Hecht wrote during the heady years of absolute studio power when stars, directors and writers were contracted to perform whatever chores the studio decreed and the producer was king. 'Writing in Hollywood,' observed the anthropologist, Hortense Powdermaker, 'can be compared to an assembly line, but one in which the assertion of an individual's ego, usually the producer's, is generally more important than the quality of the script.' Hecht complained that he spent more time arguing than writing. 'My chief memory of movieland is one of asking in the producer's office why I must change the script, eviscerate it, cripple and hamstring it? Why must I strip the hero of his few semi-intelligent remarks and why must I tack on a corny ending that makes the stomach shudder?' In those days, the producer assigned the writer, often several writers, to thrash out the screenplay. And it was to the producer that the writer submitted his various drafts. During a succession of story conferences each draft

William Goldman's adventures in the screen trade taught him that discretion is the better part of valour for the Hollywood screenwriter.

was reviewed and rewritten according to the dictates of the producer. Only then would a director be assigned, once again by the producer.

If the novice screenwriter, newly arrived in Hollywood, was in need of any guidance about how to behave during his first story conference, he could find some life-saving tips in *A Professional Manual of Screen Playwriting* (1951) by Lewis Herman. During the story conference the writer would be advised that, of course, he was entirely free to reject or accept the producer's suggestions as he saw fit. 'But if he is experienced,' counselled Herman, 'he rejects only minor changes and suggestions and accepts most of those made by his salary-superiors, the exact number of acceptances being in direct proportion to the importance of his critics in the studio hierarchy, and to the writer's desire to retain his job and to get further assignments.' Writing some thirty years after Herman published his manual of screenwriting tips, William Goldman had similar advice for the unsullied screenwriter attending his first story conference: 'There is one crucial rule that must be followed in all creative meetings:

Never speak first. At least at the start, your job is to shut up.'
Plus ça change.

The demise of the studios and the collapse of the contract system liberated writers from their servitude to the producer. But this new liberty was akin to that of the slave who is free to work for a new master on terms only a little less onerous than those which prevailed under the old regime. The emancipation of the creative talent – writers, directors, stars – which had once been under contract to the studios, like so many revolutionary movements before and since, ushered in a new, deceptively egalitarian world in which some were more equal than others and the writer was less equal than any.

The extinction of the contract system opened up a host of new opportunities for directors and stars, opportunities they and their agents lost little time in exploiting. But the status of the newly freelanced screenwriters was not much of an improvement on that of the old contract writers chained to their Underwoods in the writer's building on the studio lot. In fact, in at least one respect, their position was worse. The screenwriters had escaped the clutches of the producer only to find themselves at the behest of a new master, the director. Under the contract system, the director had been, with few exceptions, the producer's pawn, one among many. Now he came into his own. And a new weapon – critical orthodoxy – was added to the formidable arsenal arraigned against the beleaguered screenwriter.

La politique des auteurs was a theory first propounded in 1954 by the French director, François Truffaut. In the journal he founded with a group of like-minded filmmaker-critics, *Cahiers du cinéma*, Truffaut wrote that the director was king. It was the director who was the true author of the film. It was his personality, his beliefs that gave the film its original stamp. The *auteur* theory was taken up with gusto by some of America's most influential critics – notably, Andrew

Gore Vidal dismisses the majority of studio era directors as, at best, bright technicians.

Sarris of *The Village Voice* in New York – and, in Hollywood, the status of the director soared to stellar heights. Much to his surprise, the director, formerly a conscientious character actor, found himself cast in a starring role. Naturally, few screenwriters subscribed to the new fan club. 'With certain exceptions,' wrote Gore Vidal of his years as a contract writer to MGM, 'the directors were, at worst, brothers-in-law; at best, bright technicians. All in all, they were a cheery, unpretentious lot, and if anyone had told them that they were *auteurs du cinéma*, few could have coped with the concept, much less the French.'

Now, according to this newly minted gospel from across the ocean, these 'hustler-plagiarists', as Vidal called them, were 'autonomous and original artists.' But if the director was the author, where did that leave the poor writer? Answer: as powerless as before except that now writers found themselves robbed even of their nominal identity as authors. Of course, the anonymity of the screenwriters did nothing to diminish the indispensability of what they wrote. Carl Foreman succinctly expressed the chagrin of a legion of scribes when he likened the ludicrous sight of 'a director without a screenplay he can *auteur*' to 'a Don Juan without a penis'. And William Goldman remembers the moment he was first told about the existence of the *auteur* theory. 'I listened and listened as the explanation went on, and all I could think of was this: "What's the punch line?"'

Even so, the directorial possessive became the norm in Hollywood and everywhere else. In 1964, Gore Vidal arrived at the Cannes Film Festival to collect the critics' award for his script for *The Best Man*, only to discover that the movie which he had written, adapted in fact from his own play, was billed as *Un film de Franklin Schaffner*. 'Well, I just hit the ceiling. I mean, this was my play, my movie. I had helped put the thing together; I had hired Frank. "*Un film de Franklin Schaffner!*"'

And that directorial possessive is confirmed in the public mind by the fact that every magazine writer, newspaper critic and television pundit who covers cinema in any way adopts it almost exclusively. 'The public knows more about the director than anyone else because film critics, in order to be able to write reviews, apparently have to personalize and channel the creative forces into one person,' says the veteran screenwriter, Ernest Lehman, who among many other credits wrote *North by Northwest*. 'It's just too difficult for them, or too much work for them, to review a film and find out who did what to whom.' The implication being, whoever may be doing whatever to whomever else, the writer can be sure that someone, somewhere is doing it to him.

Hollywood eats writers for breakfast. But before the meal, comes the business of choosing which writers should be placed on the daily menu. In order to process the massive quantity of screenplays offered to the studios each year, far more than can be read by the harassed corps of busy development executives, professional readers are hired to assess the material. Reading screenplays is a skill which many studio executives do not possess. According to Ernest Lehman, 'Most people aren't capable of reading a screenplay and knowing that, even though it seems to be well *written*, on *paper*, it might make a bad *picture*. It's a very difficult thing to spot.' Studio executives will sometimes go to extreme lengths to avoid having to read a screenplay. One writer tells the story of an executive who asked her if she could submit her screenplay on an audio cassette so he could listen to it in the car on his way to work. Most executives escape the chore by employing professionals to read for them.

Readers are like professional tasters who are employed to ascertain if a certain type of food will agree with their employer's digestive system. And like professional tasters, whose job it is to put their own stomachs on the line every day, the working life of an average reader tends to be quite brief. Burn-outs are frequent. Readers have to wade through ten to fifteen scripts a week to make a living and the consequences of subjecting themselves to such a volume of dreck inevitably takes its toll. Stan Chervin is a story editor at Tri-Star Pictures who cut his teeth as a reader. 'The freelance reader is the infantry of the development wars, the front line defending the space on a studio executive's desk,' he says. 'Only in the film industry is so much responsibility handed over to those at the very *bottom* of the pyramid.' Herschel Weingrod, one of the writers on *Kindergarten Cop*, started his career as a reader. In retrospect he is alarmed at the degree of power he had despite his relative youth and inexperience. 'I suddenly had the power to say, "No", although I didn't have the power to say, "Yes". I had a stack of screenplays and if I rejected them, they never got past me to the next tier of authority. It frightened me to have that kind of power.' The important characteristic about 'coverage' – the reader's report on a screenplay – is that it is the only time someone commits an opinion in writing. According to Chervin, 'because it's in writing, it stays around. The readers will come and go. The executives will come and go. But that coverage is put in a drawer somewhere, and if the script comes back five years later, they'll pull out that piece of paper.'

'The best readers,' says Lindsay Doran, 'are those who are most definitely not aspiring or frustrated screenwriters. It's really easy when you are trying to make it as a writer to put down everybody else's stuff. I don't like readers who aren't compassionate.' Readers are supposed to read a screenplay with their critical faculties unencumbered, to taste the screenplay with a clean palate, as it were. But sometimes coverage can be confused by political considerations. Many readers learn that it is in their interests to trim their comments to the tastes of their employers. Production executives choose readers whose taste mirrors their own. And junior development executives will sometimes coach a reader or encourage the reader to revise the coverage before passing it on to their superior. There are even examples of readers being fired for refusing to change their coverage to support an executive's pet project.

The reader's report follows a simple format. At the top of the front page comes the basic information about the screenplay: title, author, length, genre and 'elements attached'. This last category refers to any interest in or commitment to the script that might have been expressed by an actor or director. If the elements attached are bankable, say a star or a successful director, then the rest of the coverage is academic. 'The coverage doesn't have as much value as who submitted it, who else is interested in it, or how much passion or lack thereof the studio executive has for that script,' says Chervin.

In other words, politics matter. If the screenplay is being submitted by a powerful director or a star or if the script happens to be a particular executive's pet project, then whatever the reader might have to say is largely meaningless.

Following on from the submission information, comes the 'log line'. This is a one- or two-sentence summary of the plot. The log line for *Tootsie* might have been as follows: 'An unemployed actor disguises himself as a woman to get a job on a soap opera'; or for *Back to the Future*: 'A teenager travels back to 1955 in order to get his parents together before he ceases to exist.' Movies that can be readily condensed in this way are known as 'high concept'. The log line for a character study like *Driving Miss Daisy* – 'The twenty-year relationship between a black chauffeur and his Jewish employer' – tells you very little about the movie. On the other hand, 'three entrepreneurs set up a business to get rid of ghosts in Manhattan', tells you everything you need to know about *Ghostbusters*. High-concept movies, such as this one, are traditionally beloved by studio executives because they can be easily and accurately summarized in thirty seconds, which is the average running time for a television commercial. So, high-concept movies are easy to sell and, as a consequence, the few, choice words that make up the log line may well be the reader's most significant contribution because they may be the *only* words the studio executive bothers to read.

As significant as the log line and as easily digestible is the score box at the bottom of the page where the reader is asked to rate the script in several areas – premise, story line, character, dialogue, setting, production values. The reader places a tick (excellent, good, fair or poor) against each category. There may also be a budget line at the bottom where the reader will have to estimate the movie's budget although nobody else's opinion counts for as little in this regard as the reader's. Then comes a one- or two-page synopsis followed by a half page of comments and the reader's final recommendation once again expressed as a tick against one of three boxes: 'Recommend' (or 'I'd spend my own money to make this movie'), 'Consider' ('I'd spend your money to make this movie'), or 'Pass' ('You couldn't pay me to see this movie').

According to Lindsay Doran, 'The best reason to read coverage is to find out what the concept is. A lot of executives are looking for high-concept material and that's why they read the coverage first. But I find that coverage never tells me what I need to know. Frequently it misses the great idea.' Although the anonymous reader may be the only sympathetic audience the writer ever gets, the submission process favours the acceptance of simple, recognizable plots and characters and encourages the rejection of scripts dealing with complex ideas in an original way. Well before it is swallowed by the studio and enters the digestive system, the presentation of the screenplay has been processed, diluted or flavoured to cater to what the reader assumes is the studio's taste. 'It's very hard through the coverage process ever to find anything wonderful. It's too watered down,' says Lindsay Doran.

Screenwriters worry that once their script has been covered, no executive will ever bother to read the original screenplay. 'If you want somebody to respond favourably to your script, and there's unfavourable coverage, then you've got a problem,' admits Chervin. Most executives will admit that coverage is not a foolproof process but they rely on it all the same. Each studio makes around fifteen movies a year. The studio may have, on average, about 100 scripts in development, which have been selected from the 4000 or so submissions the studio receives each year. 'Somebody's got to read them,' says Chervin, 'and it's better that it be a reader, who can devote his full attention from the first page to the last page, than some studio executive who'll just read ten pages before deciding he doesn't like it.' Most people – executives and writers alike – accept the system as a necessary evil.

If the writer is fortunate and the coverage is appetizing, the studio executive is likely to order up the full meal and the lucky screenplay will begin its passage through the studio's digestive tract, otherwise known as the development process. The development process is notorious. 'I went through numerous development meetings,' says the screenwriter and director, Oliver Stone, whose movies include *Platoon, Salvador, Wall Street* and *Born on the Fourth of July*. 'The studios have committees of people, college-educated types, who sit around a table and tell you what's wrong with your script. And it's always the same thing. They always hit the same beats: the character's not sympathetic; he's not in jeopardy; the third act doesn't work ... There's a routine set of lines they use. I just find it debilitating. The resulting script is a compromise. I've seen writers destroyed by that system.' In general, the more people who are involved in the development process, the more edges the script may once have had will be worn off, the more you will get something that resembles the work of a committee than the vision of any single person. According to Howard Rodman, 'A lot of these people don't really understand that you can write on blank paper. They only know how to write on paper that somebody else has already written on. They seriously assume that their role is to save the writer from his or her worst impulses towards self-destructiveness and non-commerciality. They want to come in and fix it up.'

At some point, a writer has to decide whether to give in to the way the system works or make some kind of stand. Fighting words sound good but essentially writers who want to *do* something about the way they are treated have only two options open to them. The first is for the writer to ally him or herself to a powerful director.

The other is to become a director. Roger Simon works with somebody who has control, director Paul Mazursky. Simon and Mazursky co-authored the screenplay for *Enemies, A Love Story* (for which they were nominated for an Academy Award) and they are currently working together on other projects. 'You either have to be in control or in partnership with somebody who knows you're doing the right thing and who has control,' says Simon. 'Otherwise, forget it.'

Writer Kurt Luedtke has worked consistently with director Sydney Pollack. They may not always agree with one another but at least they speak the same language and Pollack has the muscle to ensure that whatever they decide will be accepted by the studio. Luedtke recalls that they had a particularly vigorous discussion about the character played by Sally Field in *Absence of Malice*. Field played a reporter who had written a story that had indirectly caused a suicide. There is a scene in which she has to confront the suicide victim's best friend, who is played by Paul Newman. 'There was a feeling that the female character should apologize and I felt very strongly that she should not apologize,' says Luedtke. 'Journalistically, there wasn't anything wrong with what she had done, and if she apologized it made her smaller as a person. I don't like to see the woman characters getting pushed around for the sake of the male character.' That was an argument that Luedtke won. But the point is that he was working with a director with whom he had a relationship of mutual respect and trust.

As for Phil Alden Robinson, his bruising experience on *Rhinestone* taught him a valuable lesson. 'If I'm going to be a writer in this business,' he says, 'I'm going to exercise some kind of creative control.' Robinson not only wrote but also directed his next movie, *Field of Dreams*. He became a hyphenate. A hyphenate is someone who fulfils more than a single creative role in the making of a movie. So a writer who also directs or produces or both is a hyphenate. The

Kurt Luedtke won his battle to prevent journalist Sally Field from apologizing to Paul Newman in Absence of Malice *(right).*

term derives from the writer's most potent punctuation mark – the hyphen – that links the roles, writer-producer, writer-director, writer-producer-director, or as Mel Brooks defines the term, 'writer-producer-director-out-of-work.' At a single stroke, the writer's liabilities are transformed into assets. A writer-director or a writer-producer is a formidable combination. A writer-director-producer in one breathing body is virtually indestructible. Not only do they have access to what everyone in Hollywood craves – original screenplays – but they are in a position to do something about it. No writer *on his own* has sufficient weight to muscle a movie into production but a writer with a bankable screenplay, one that is clearly commercial and that *everybody wants to buy,* can parlay the property into a chance

to direct. And if the film is successful, the newly minted writer-director is on his way. 'Once a writer directs his or her first film and it's an artistic and/or a commercial success,' says agent, Peter Benedek, 'then the sky's the limit.'

The hyphenate is not a new phenomenon. Preston Sturges and John Huston were both notable writers turned writer-directors; Paddy Chayefsky and Ernest Lehman opted to become writer-producers. But the metamorphosis of writers into hyphenates of one kind or another can now be seen with unprecedented frequency – Oliver Stone, David Mamet, John Milius and many more have become writer-directors. It was his original screenplays that enabled

George Lucas to elevate himself to the status of writer-director and then a writer-director-producer. And this ploy is not restricted to writers who wish to direct. Sylvester Stallone converted the asset he possessed in the form of the screenplay for *Rocky* into an opportunity to star in the movie.

James Orr is another brand-new writer-director. With his partner, Jim Cruickshank (they've been writing together since 1978), he wrote the phenomenally successful movie, *Three Men and a Baby* for Disney. Again with Cruickshank, he co-authored their next screenplay, *Mr Destiny*, a fairy tale in a similar vein to Frank Capra's *It's a Wonderful Life* in which, through heavenly intervention, a beaten man comes to terms with his life as it is. But this time Orr also directed. Orr very deliberately chose to write his own material as a way to lever himself into a position where he would be able to direct. 'I decided that the single best way to direct movies was to write them. He who controls the material has got all the cards. If you have a piece of material someone wants, you may not get to direct instantly but you have a great deal of leverage to build to that point.'

From the studio's point of view, hyphenates also mean greater efficiency. The business of studio production involves the harnessing of various creative elements to a given project. Securing the services of the writer and the director can involve protracted negotiations with their respective agents. If the writer and director are one and the same person, that process of negotiation becomes simpler. As Orr says 'As soon as you are a hyphenate and you are combining more than one function, and you do it successfully, not only can you consolidate that much creative power in one person but you also make the studio executive's job easier.'

In some cases, the power that naturally accrues to the director can be so intoxicating that many writers who go on to direct tend to forsake their origins. They cease writing and become directors of other writers' screenplays. The prolific filmmaker, Oliver Stone, is an exception. Stone achieved his early recognition as a screenwriter when he won an Academy Award for *Midnight Express*, and since then he has always written his own material, either alone or in collaboration with another writer. 'I was always a writer. I love writing. Physically, I find it the most relaxing time of my life. You have no people around.' During the summer of 1990, while Stone was editing and scoring *Born on the Fourth of July*, he was also writing the screenplay for his next film, *The Doors*, based on the life of the rock and roll icon, Jim Morrison. In the morning, Stone would write for five hours or so, alone in his study, and in the afternoon he would work with the editors. 'I've been able to combine writing with editing a lot. They are similar. They are both quieter activities.'

Few filmmakers exemplify so well the way by which a writer can convert his liabilities into assets by directing his own work. Writing is intrinsic to Stone's survival as a filmmaker. 'I know the material better when I have it on the page,' he says. 'I have to be involved in the script to really fully understand it. The idea is king. If I have the idea and the idea is good, it will work. Knowing that gives me a certain strength. I don't depend on a system to get a movie made.' Stone approaches filmmaking as if he were fighting a war and his tactics for survival are instructive to any writer who wants to beat the odds and get through the Hollywood jungle without being branded, 'Missing in Action'.

'The writing is important to me because that's where you set your vision, the spine of the material,' says Stone. 'And you've got to stick to the spine because it's going to be a hell of a bumpy ride and you're going to want to get off several times. You're not facing good odds – most films are failures – and the chances are you're going to get wiped out along the way. You've got to be able to bounce back. You're going to take a lot of blows and you're going to have to make the movie against all these objections. Every step along the way they're going to be pressurizing you to compromise your vision, so you've got to know what's in your gut, what you believe in. You're going to have to be like a Sherman tank.'

Stone's tactics have proven themselves effective. Among the screenwriter's limited arsenal, his methodology is the equivalent of a nuclear capability. It is the ultimate deterrent. But Stone is exceptional. Few writers have the capacity to mount such an offensive. The ones who survive know that the odds are stacked against them and they adapt accordingly. They are outnumbered and outgunned. Their ammunition is limited. They have to resort to guerrilla tactics. They must choose their own ground and content themselves with picking off selected targets when the opportunity arises. Above all they must ensure they have the right friends. Screenwriters can never win the war, but they can hold their own if they have the right allies. Because they do not have the brawn, they must adopt the alternative option: it's the survival of the smartest.

CHAPTER FIVE

HUSTLER-ARTISTS

In order to make a motion picture, you must have money. And in order to have money, you've got to woo people. And in order to woo people, you've got to bullshit 'em.

Samuel Fuller, director

It's a seller's market. The studios desperately need product and that puts directors in a stronger position than they have ever known.

Sydney Pollack, director

You get your very own canvas-backed chair with your name scrawled across the back. You get to say, 'Action!' and 'Cut!' You get to meet famous and beautiful people who depend on your advice and skill. You get laid a lot. You get interviewed by earnest young critics from across the ocean who want to know the sub-text of something that probably wasn't your own idea and which you never understood in the first place. So you get to improvize, on and off set. In short, you get to have a fun time. And you get paid a king's ransom to do it. It's no wonder that the T-shirt which announces to the world, 'What I really want to do is direct', is such a best-seller. Short of movie stardom, and some directors are stars too, it's the most glamorous occupation in the world.

At least, that's the popular myth. Of course, as every director who has ever addressed a class of eager film students will tell you, there's a hitch. 'It's tough to become a director and once you've made it, it's murder to stay there. You have to suffer for your art,' the director will say with a sad little smile. 'It's not in the least bit glamorous.' The students nod knowingly. 'On location, the problems can seem insurmountable. The hours are terrible. The anxieties are guaranteed to give you ulcers.' The students look sympathetic. 'And if anything goes wrong, if the movie is a disaster, you are the one who's responsible. It's your fault, and yours alone. It's a killing job,' says the director with grave finality. The students look grim. They don't believe a word he's saying. They want to make movies. They want to make a fortune. They're besotted by the glamour. They're in for a surprise because everything the veteran director has told them is true: directing really is murderously exhausting work.

'It's like being a doctor,' says George Lucas, the director of *American Graffiti* and *Star Wars*. 'You work long hours, very hard hours, and it's emotional, tense work. If you don't really love it, then it ain't worth it.' When a movie is in production, directors routinely work long hours beginning at 5.00 in the morning and going through to 10.00 or 11.00 at night. 'Between setting up, looking at dailies, preparing for the next day's filming it's really non-stop,' says Ivan Reitman, who has directed and produced a string of top-grossing comedies. 'Once production begins, the day is interminable. The demands by the crew are never-ending. There's a hundred people with a hundred different problems and a hundred different decisions that have to be made. There are actors whose egos have to be massaged. There are constant script problems that never seem to die. And you finally get home; you haven't seen your children for a week and you haven't spoken more than three words to your wife but you really have to review the next day's work because the thing continues.'

Sydney Pollack, director of more than a dozen movies, including *Tootsie*, *Out of Africa* and, more recently, *Havana*, is in no doubt about what it takes to direct movies. 'The most important thing,' he says, 'is to be in good physical shape. It's the most enormously gruelling physical exercise, partly because there is so much emotional strain. For every moment that it takes you to solve the artistic problem, it's costing millions of dollars. And millions of dollars make people behave badly. Grown men behave like five-year-olds. They cry. They threaten you. They get hysterical.' When David Mamet, the playwright and screenwriter, made his directorial début on the movie *House of Games*, he tried to stack the odds in his favour by working with a cast and crew whom he knew and trusted, and by planning every detail of what was a modestly budgeted movie well in advance. Even so, by the end of each day he was so tired that driving home he hit the same tree three nights in a row. 'I would arrive home, thank God I hadn't fallen asleep on the way, take my foot off the brake and start out of the car, and the car, which was still in drive, would proceed into the tree.'

The fears and frustrations that can assail a filmmaker during production have been recorded in vivid detail by John Boorman, the director of *Point Blank*, *Deliverance* and *Excalibur*, who kept a journal while he was making *The Emerald Forest* on location in the middle of the Brazilian rain forests. In Boorman's case, the tremendous logistical problems of making the movie were compounded by the erratic behaviour of his financiers in Britain and America. The journal runs from June 1982, when Boorman first conceived the idea for the movie, to March 1985 when the film was finally completed. It makes ghoulish reading: 'We are having terrible problems getting the equipment out of customs ... Our transport is in disarray ... The deal is still not concluded ... Our preparations are falling behind schedule ... Costs are escalating in an alarming way ... The production is still in chaos: most of our camera and grip equipment is still held by customs ... The first two weeks have

Heart of darkness: John Boorman overcame daunting obstacles to film The Emerald Forest *in Brazil.*

been horrendous. It has rained every day, sometimes without respite. We just try to keep shooting, but it is miserable. We are way behind schedule, and we just cannot seem to stem the haemorrhaging budget ... The crew's morale is low ... I am two weeks behind schedule ... It is still raining most of the time. Of course, the locals say they have never seen anything like it for forty years ... horrendously tough ... We finally reached Tucurui to discover that the freight plane carrying our equipment had broken down in Rio ... We are still waiting for it to arrive ... We are all exhausted ... continuous harassment from Embassy [Boorman's American financiers] ... They treat us as adversaries.' And finally, 'Yesterday was our last day of shooting ... The pressure will be off and I can function like a normal human being.'

Boorman's chronicle of woe shows the depth of motivation and commitment that directing movies requires. Nevertheless, no matter how draining the work may be, many people who are not film students, who already work in the movie business, who should know better, desperately want to direct. Why? Because beyond glamour, directing offers what everyone who works in the movie business secretly craves: control. Writers who are tired of being rewritten, stars who are sick of being type-cast, cinematographers and editors who have had just about enough of seeing their artistry credited to others: they all want to direct because they want to keep control of their own work. Francis Coppola, John Milius, Oliver Stone, Robert Towne and David Mamet are all directors who started out as writers. Paul Mazursky and Sydney Pollack were actors before they became directors. Robert Redford, Clint Eastwood, Jack Nicholson and Barbra Streisand shift back and forth between acting and directing. Nicolas Roeg, Ridley Scott and Haskell Wexler were cameramen first. Hal Ashby and David Lean began as editors. They all opted to direct because directing gives you the power to do whatever you want to do, assuming that the weather, riots or the indecision of your financiers do not stand in your way.

Directors have not always enjoyed such power. Although movies began as a director's medium, from the twenties onwards and for most of Hollywood's history directors have been subservient to the studio, the producer or the star. 'When the industry was young, the filmmaker was at its core and the man who handled the business details his partner,' remarked George Stevens, the director of *Shane* and *Giant*. 'When he finally looked around, he found his partner's name on the door. Thus the filmmaker became the employee, and the man who had time to attend to the business details became the head of the studio.' In 1919, the greatest of Hollywood's early directors, D. W. Griffith, tried to escape the studio's leash when he joined Mary Pickford, Charles Chaplin and Douglas Fairbanks to form United Artists. Griffith, who did so much to define the vocabulary of filmmaking when he directed the very first full-length feature, *Birth of a Nation*, chaffed against the growing power of the studios. United Artists represented his bid for independence. But the dream foundered because Griffith and his partners failed to make a sufficient number of movies each year to make the studio profitable. Within little more than a decade, Griffith's huge personal debts had forced him to sell out and his career was over.

Griffith's bid for independence failed and his fellow directors were left to fight a rear-guard action for autonomy within the emerging studio system, in which the power was wielded by the head of production. The two sides were mismatched from the start, as the ferocious battle between Erich von Stroheim and Irving Thalberg showed only too well. In the early twenties, Erich von Stroheim, who wrote, directed and often starred in his movies, personified the director as autocrat. Von Stroheim was on contract to Universal when a new production chief, Irving Thalberg, arrived on the lot. Thalberg's policy was to leave his directors alone during shooting, but he took a close personal interest in the scripting, budgeting and cutting of the movies he supervised. Von Stroheim and Thalberg first clashed in 1921 when the director presented Thalberg with a three-and-a-half-hour-long sex farce, *Foolish Wives*, which he had made for the then astronomical sum of over $1 million. When von Stroheim refused to recut the picture, Thalberg locked him out of the editing rooms and made the necessary cuts himself. Subsequently von Stroheim left Universal to make *Greed* for Sam Goldwyn, but by the time this movie was complete Goldwyn was on the point of merging his studio with Louis B. Mayer to form MGM. Von Stroheim's seven-hour masterpiece then fell under the supervision of MGM's new production chief who, as fate would have it, was

Von Stroheim directs Greed, *blissfully unaware that his seven-hour masterpiece was destined to be butchered by MGM's new production chief, Irving Thalberg.*

none other than the pesky Thalberg. When von Stroheim refused to cut the picture down to less than four hours, Thalberg simply instructed another director, Rex Ingram, to do the work. Even though Ingram cut the movie by an hour, Thalberg cut it down still further to standard length.

The coming of sound, which cemented moviemaking as a studio-based enterprise, meant that the studio and the producer had the upper hand and directors had to conform to an established system of production. Pandro S. Berman, the producer of such movies as *Top Hat* and *The Blackboard Jungle*, recalls that in Louis B. Mayer's day, directors were routinely considered to be expendable. 'Some-times you'd have one director on a picture for a while, and if he got sick, instead of calling the picture off for a week as they would now if Mike Nichols took ill, they'd say, "Jack Conway isn't well. Let him rest. We'll put Harry Beaumont on it for a week, and he'll pick up where Jack left off". That's the way we made pictures.' Of course, some directors were able to make highly individual, idiosyncratic movies within the studio system, but the source of power was still

A risky moment for Cary Grant in North by Northwest *but no worries for the director. Alfred Hitchcock received a fee of $250 000 plus a share of the box-office takings.*

clearly understood. The studios could accommodate mavericks but the bosses' tolerance for such untamed talents was in direct proportion to the commercial success of their movies.

During the studio era and even after, the director who exploited the system with the most conspicuous success was Alfred Hitchcock. During Hitchcock's early years in Hollywood he had been severely constrained, probably for the better, by the supervision of producer, David O. Selznick, who had brought the British director to Hollywood and put him under contract. But by the early fifties, Hitchcock had developed his own distinctive style to such a degree that it had become a trademark as effective in drawing audiences as any star name. By the end of the fifties, after the contract system had toppled, he was able to strike a deal for making movies that compared favourably with the terms of most stars. For directing *North by Northwest*, he received a fee of $250 000 plus 10 per cent of the movie's gross receipts above $8 million. And by 1962, Hitchcock was the third-largest stockholder in MCA, the owners of Universal.

In 1954, Hitchcock's status in particular, and that of directors in general, received an added boost from an unexpected source. A young French critic, François Truffaut, published an article in the film journal, *Cahiers du cinéma*, which attributed a movie's authorship to the director alone. Truffaut's *Politique des auteurs* was shared by his colleagues at *Cahiers* – Godard, Chabrol, Rohmer, Rivette and others. They were all aspiring directors themselves, so their theories were conveniently self-serving. As the American film critic, David Thomson, has observed, 'In France, above all, the young critics hailed distinguished veterans because they wanted to be like them ... The definition of the role of director was a description of a task and a splendour that Truffaut, Godard and the others wanted for themselves.' It invariably takes time for a wary Hollywood to accept ideas from Europe but once American critics had opted to take the *auteur* theory to their hearts, it wasn't long before Hollywood followed suit. Directors, who for years had been domesticated by the studios, were lionized. However, whereas the *Cahiers* critics had never applied the theory indiscriminately but more as a measure by which some directors were elevated above others, in Hollywood, there was little inclination to be so discerning. Suddenly all directors were hot.

The *auteur* theory was well-timed. It catered to the aspirations of a new generation of filmmakers who barged into Hollywood in the sixties – Francis Coppola, George Lucas, Martin Scorsese, John Milius, Brian De Palma and Steven Spielberg. Most of them were film-school graduates who were primed to make movies their own way. And the phenomenal commercial success of their films – Coppola's *The Godfather, Parts I* and *II,* Lucas's *American Graffiti* and *Star Wars,* Spielberg's *Jaws* and *Close Encounters of the Third Kind* – gave them an unprecedented degree of leverage. 'We are the pigs,' announced George Lucas. 'We are the ones who sniff out the truffles. You can put us on a leash, keep us under control. But we are the guys who dig out the gold. The man in the executive tower cannot do that ... They know as much about making movies as a banker does ... But the power lies with us – the ones who actually know how to make movies.'

Lucas, Coppola, Milius and their ilk represented a new genus of filmmaker – they were hustler-artists, who understood the commercial realities of making and marketing movies and used that knowledge to buttress their independence. 'Nobody in a studio challenges the final cut of a film now,' John Milius said at the time. 'I think they realize the filmmakers are likely to be around a lot longer than the studio executives.'

In particular, Coppola, Spielberg and Lucas made the system work for them to an astounding degree. In a sense, and almost accidentally, they achieved what D. W. Griffith had dreamed of forty years before –

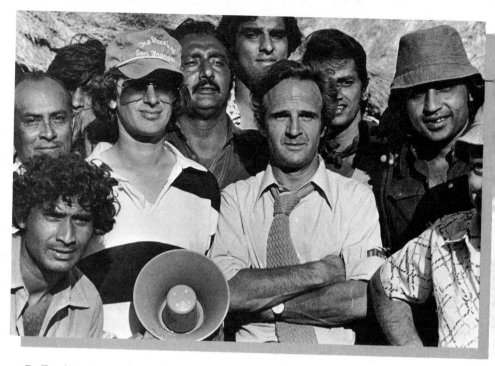

Dr Frankenstein meets his monster: François Truffaut, who coined the auteur *theory,
on the set of* Close Encounters of the Third Kind *with movie brat Steven Spielberg,
who took him at his word.*

they became, each in their own way, moguls. *Jaws, Close Encounters
of the Third Kind, ET,* and the three Indiana Jones movies have made
Spielberg the most successful director in the history of motion
pictures. And through his company, Amblin Entertainment, he has
shepherded the movies of a new generation of directors such as
Robert Zemeckis (*Who Framed Roger Rabbit?, Back to the Future, Parts
I, II and III*), and Joe Dante (*Gremlins, Parts I and II*). But Spielberg
is first and foremost a director. He is at heart a reluctant mogul. So
too, one senses, is George Lucas, although perhaps more than
anyone, he epitomizes the hustler-artist. In Hollywood, Lucas is
renowned for his ability to cut 'killer deals'. It's an ability which has
become mandatory for director-producers since the demise of the
studio system. When he was negotiating to make *Star Wars* for
Twentieth Century Fox, Lucas persuaded the studio to give him
control of the movie's merchandizing rights as well as control of any

future sequels in return for paying a smaller fee upfront. The value of those concessions never occurred to the Fox executives but in time the proceeds from the deal were to generate $30 million for Lucas's company, Lucasfilm, guaranteeing him an extraordinary degree of autonomy which he went on to exploit as a producer. Subsequent revenues from *The Empire Strikes Back* and *Return of the Jedi* have allowed him to build a 2600-acre production complex, Skywalker Ranch. Lucas has put his own money into many of the movies he has made although he continues to depend on the majors to distribute them. Even so, like Spielberg, Lucas is a reluctant mogul who has drawn back from trying to expand too far. The same cannot be said for Francis Coppola. Of the three, he is the only one who truly sought and relished the role of mogul.

A garrulous, passionate cinephile, Coppola was making movies in Hollywood even before he had finished his studies at UCLA filmschool. Coppola met George Lucas while making *Finian's Rainbow* for Warners. Lucas worked with Coppola on his next project, *The Rain People*, an intimate road movie that Coppola wrote, directed and made on the move, gypsy-style, with a close-knit cast and crew. Equipped, according to Coppola, 'with just a few cars and an editing table in a bus', he started out from New York, without a complete script, and effectively made the movie up over four months as he and his team travelled west as far as Nebraska. The improvisational, family style of making *The Rain People* far away from Hollywood, appealed so much to Coppola that he opted to institutionalize his independence by setting up his own alternative studio in San Francisco.

American Zoetrope, with Coppola as owner and Lucas as vice-president, was founded in 1969. The aim was that the studio would attract 'the most gifted and youthful talent' around, 'using the most contemporary techniques and equipment possible'. But the next year, the new model studio foundered when Warners, which had agreed to provide financing, rejected the projects Coppola had developed for them. Among Coppola and his intimates the day was memorialized as Black Thursday. Then the success of *The Godfather* and *The Godfather, Part II* revitalized Coppola's fortunes and Zoetrope rose from the ashes. In 1979, Coppola bought a ten-and-a-half-acre studio complex in Los Angeles, equipped with nine sound stages and thirty-four editing rooms. He planned to revive the ethos of the old studios, including the signing of actors to multi-picture contracts. The dream was never fully realized. Coppola found himself sucked into the making of *Apocalypse Now*. And no sooner had he emerged from that ordeal, he was plunged into *One from the Heart*, a romantic musical which he chose to film on the Zoetrope sound stages rather than on location, a decision which eventually caused the movie's

Heart attack: Nastassia Kinski in One from the Heart, *the movie that forced Francis Coppola to file for bankruptcy.*

budget to blossom from $15 million to more than $26 million. The box-office failure of *One from the Heart* eventually forced Coppola to file for bankruptcy.

But if Coppola failed to sustain himself as a mogul, he has succeeded in surviving appalling odds as a filmmaker. The making of *Apocalypse Now*, on location in the Philippines during the typhoon season, was an unremitting nightmare for him. 'There were times,' he says, 'when I thought I was going to die, literally, from the inability to move the problems I had. I would go to bed at four in the morning in a cold sweat.' The strain proved too much for actor Martin Sheen, who suffered a near-fatal heart attack. Problems continued to dog Coppola well into post-production. The release of the movie, originally scheduled for December 1977, was delayed for two years as Coppola struggled to cut together one and a half million feet of film. 'In Hollywood they would have burned me alive in three days. I started filming without a finished script, and I've gone double over budget, and it's taken twice as long just to edit the film.'

In the event, *Apocalypse Now* was commercially successful. However, it marked the first of a string of big-budget movies that were deemed to have gone dangerously out of control and which prompted studio executives to take a tougher line with their more headstrong directors. The spectacular failure of *1941*, Steven Spielberg's $34 million World War II comedy, showed that even Hollywood's Golden Boy was fallible. And when *Heaven's Gate*, a lavish western from the Academy Award-winning director of *The Deer Hunter*, Michael Cimino, went so far out of control that it forced United Artists out of business, fiscal responsibility became the order of the day.

In the aftermath of this crop of conspicuously expensive failures, a new sobriety descended on the executive suites of the studios and most directors felt an obligation to atone for the excesses of some of their more wayward colleagues by bringing their movies in on schedule and on budget. There were exceptions of course – Coppola's *The Cotton Club*, a vain attempt to repeat the success of *The Godfather*, went through thirty-eight rewrites and cost its financiers $40 million, which was some $22 million more than they had originally bargained for. But most directors, mindful of Hollywood's bottom-line fixation, are now respectful of budgets. 'It comes down to how much money you get,' says Martin Scorsese. 'That is automatically the ultimate restraint. You know, you have to be a little smarter and learn how to survive with no money. It's almost like a chess game. Every shot becomes a move in a chess game.' Scorsese only kept overall control of *The Last Temptation of Christ*, even when he delivered a finished movie of two hours and forty-six minutes, because he stayed within the modest $7.5-million budget specified by Universal.

But even though directors, like everyone else in the movie business, are ultimately constrained by the bottom line, they enjoy a privileged position. It's not easy to fire them. Writers come and go. Producers can be displaced. Directors, up to a point, are protected. Too many people are dependent on them. Before the actual physical process of shooting the movie can begin, the script has to be in shape, the cast and crew have to be chosen, the locations have to be decided upon. The physical process of making movies is fiendishly elaborate and it is very rare for a director to be thrown off a movie once it is in production. Once filming gets underway, once the army of actors and technicians and supply services are on the march, there are countless decisions every day that fall to the one and only person who can answer them, the director. 'I like to make decisions, and I like to be at the centre of things,' said David Mamet of his first time out as a director, 'but this was a bit too much of a good thing.'

The corollary to all this responsibility is authority. The cast,

The birth of a hyphenate: David Mamet makes his début at the helm, directing his wife, Lindsay Crouse, in House of Games.

the crew, the money are all held in sway to one figure. A film unit requires precise organization. It is run by a hierarchy which culminates in a sharp pinnacle. There stands the director. His or her authority is absolute. The director's word is law. It is perhaps for this reason that Robert Altman considers that ego is the greatest trap for any director. All that power can make you heady. 'The amount of deference with which one is treated is *awesome*,' says Mamet. 'One is deferred to by the crew because of the legitimate necessity of the chain of command in this sort of enterprise, and by a great deal of the outside world because of supposed and real abilities to bestow favours, contracts, jobs, orders, et cetera ... The downside of all that jolly deference and courtesy one receives as a film director is, of course, that one has to *direct* the movie.'

In some ways, making movies is a circular process. Often it might progress something like this: The movie is spawned by an idea, nurtured in solitude by a writer, developed further through an intimate collaboration between writer and director, then, once production begins the process blooms into a cross between a military campaign and an industrial plant. The writer-director Robert Towne says that going from writing to directing is like going from 'that incredible silence under water' to the surface and 'that gaggle of sound' where the noise can be deafening. And then it's all over, the movie has been shot, the crew disperse, and the cans of film are stacked along the walls of an edit suite for the director and the editor to work on in privacy. Silence returns.

The writing and editing are often blissfully contemplative by comparison to the grind of physical production, which requires from the director a mixture of ruthless determination and political acumen. The job of the director is sometimes likened to that of a political dictator but sometimes it pays for directors to be benign. Filmmaking is a collaborative process and although it is not a collaboration among equals, the director must motivate the cast and crew to give of their best within the allotted time. 'The essence of feature filmmaking is leadership,' says Taylor Hackford, director of *Against All Odds* and *An Officer and a Gentleman*. 'In order to get your vision onto the screen, you need to use the talents of other people.' Sydney Pollack is acutely sensitive to the politics of the production crew. 'Anybody who works with me,' he says, 'a cameraman, an editor, a writer, an actor is going to measure constantly how much freedom I take away from them.'

A hostile crew can make a director's life unbearable. George Lucas failed to win over his British crew when he made *Star Wars* at Elstree Studios outside London. Lucas, who admits in retrospect that his weakness as a director is that he 'wants to do everything', fought an on-going guerrilla war with his cameraman, Gil Taylor. Taylor was a veteran cinematographer, who among many other films had shot *Dr Strangelove*. 'The crew got upset,' Lucas later confided to his biographer, Dale Pollock. 'I ended up having to be nice to everybody, which is hard when you don't like a lot of the people.' Collaboration does not come naturally to Lucas. 'Ideally,' says his producer on *Star Wars*, Gary Kurtz, 'George would like to come up with an idea for a film, have everybody go out and shoot it, and then get all the footage in a room so he could finish the movie all by himself, without anyone else imposing their ideas on him.' The strain of making *Star Wars* was enough to ensure that it was the last movie Lucas ever directed.

David Mamet avoided the pitfalls that inevitably befall a virgin director who has to establish his authority with a crew of experienced craftsmen by making his début feature, *House of Games*, with a cast and crew of close friends. 'These people had no need to prove themselves to me, and, more important, I had no need to prove myself to them,' he wrote subsequently. 'That energy (small or large, but inevitable) that is devoted to establishing *bona fides* in an artistic collaboration between strangers ("How much does this other guy know? Can I trust him, is he going to hurt me?") was in our movie devoted to other things.'

For the director, the process of collaboration begins with the writer. Relations between writers and directors are inevitably volatile. Screenwriters are like surrogate mothers who are loath to come to terms with the unavoidable moment when they must surrender their baby to the adoptive parent. According to Taylor Hackford, a director can respond to the tender sensibilities of the writer in one of three ways. The first way is to work out a collaborative relationship with the original writer. Secondly, the director can bring in a new writer who shares his or her vision. The third and final alternative is to write the script yourself.

'Despite the inherent problems of fusing two creative points of view, I would personally always prefer to collaborate with the writer,' says Hackford. 'Unless it's an incredibily personal piece, most writers are better at putting words on the page than I am. However, I feel that I am much better at guiding them towards what will work best on the screen.'

Sydney Pollack says that most of the time it's the idea behind a screenplay he likes rather than the screenplay itself. Pollack works closely with his writers by adopting a kind of hybrid approach which combines the first and second of Taylor Hackford's three options. Pollack's screenplays are invariably the work of more than one writer but he tries, if he can, to keep the original writer closely involved rather than discarding him or her altogether. 'My job is to present the world as I see it and sometimes I can't do that without changing the input in some way,' says Pollack, who has a habit of typing out the screenplay himself before the start of production. To any writer who is tetchy about the authorial pretensions of directors this might seem like the ultimate abuse but for Pollack typing out the screenplay is a way of digesting it. 'As I'm typing it, I'm trying to direct it in a way.'

Pollack likes to work with people who trust him, and who understand that the process is collaborative. 'More often than not, we'll see the same world. Believe it or not, I've worked with writers who have had very satisfying experiences being rewritten. I mean, as opposed to shutting them out of the process, I've kept them continuously involved. With their consent I've said, "I think we need a new pair of eyes. Let's bring someone else in, and we'll all three work on it."' That someone else is likely to be David Rayfiel, a writer who has functioned as a script doctor, often uncredited, on many of Pollack's movies.

'There is a point at which it's understood and acknowledged when it's time to call David,' says Kurt Luedtke, who has written two movies for Pollack: *Absence of Malice*, starring Sally Field and Paul Newman, and *Out of Africa*, for which he and Pollack both won Academy Awards. 'I think it's usually somewhere around the third draft that we call David. What David does is as much editing as it is writing. David has a very keen eye for things that are phoney, and the first thing that happens is that the phoney things get identified. David goes off and writes; I go off and write; we often write the same scene – Sydney loves to have multiple choices. Happily enough, the three of us work well together.'

For Pollack, a lot of the work he does with writers is just hanging about together. 'You get up. You meet. You have breakfast. You wander around. You have lunch. You don't ever leave. You get very bored with each other and very short with each other sometimes. It's like an odd forced marriage. That's just the way I work and some writers don't like it.' According to Kurt Luedtke, a burst of professional married life with Sydney Pollack is a pleasant enough experience although he appreciates that not every writer might find it so congenial. 'I think it's inevitable that one or two things happen,' he says. 'You either become very good friends or the process becomes intolerable, and if it becomes intolerable, then probably the picture doesn't get made.'

Pollack's way of working is not to try to have every 'i' dotted and every 't' crossed before he starts production. He likes to leave space for the movie to evolve as he's shooting. As a result, Pollack's writers are often still working on the screenplay up to the last day of principal photography and sometimes beyond. Pollack recalls that the screenplay for *Out of Africa* was worked on continually, from the first draft, which was completed in December 1983, through to the final day of shooting, on 6 June 1985. All told the screenplay went through six or seven drafts. Pollack has lost trace of exactly how many there were.

Most directors regard the screenplay as a flexible blueprint rather than a bible. Ivan Reitman maintains that he has never filmed a scene exactly the way it was written down on the page. 'When you start to block a scene it has to change because the movement in itself points out problems or makes certain lines unnecessary,' he says. 'And I'm always looking for a way to trim things down, to make them tighter.' Oliver Stone, who began as a screenwriter and directs from screenplays he has written either alone or in collaboration with another writer, is equally pragmatic. 'I'm not very wedded to the word. I'll write it but if the actor reads it another way and changes a word here or there I have no problem with that. As a result I rewrite my dialogue quite a bit. But often, you know, I will go through a set of changes three or four or five times and at the end of the day I will pull out the first draft and say to the actor, "Look, you're saying this, exactly this". So we've made a long circle to come back to the beginning again.'

The ability to work with actors, to cast correctly, to bring out the best possible performance is one of the director's prime responsibilities. No movie will work if the audience does not feel some empathy with the protagonists on the screen although clearly some movies are more dependent on the depth and complexity of their characters than others. The characters who appear in *Star Wars*, for example, although they need to engage the audience, do not need to be compelling in the same way as the protagonists in such character-based movies as *Terms of Endearment*, *Driving Miss Daisy* or *Out of Africa*. George Lucas's biographer, Dale Pollock, notes that while making *Star Wars*, Lucas did not enjoy dealing with the actors. Mark Hamill, who played the young hero, Luke Skywalker, in the movie confessed to a sneaking suspicion 'that if there were a way to make movies without actors, George would do it'.

On the other hand Oliver Stone, who makes some of the most polemical and personal movies around, tends to identify closely

Never again: George Lucas on the set of Star Wars *with Alec Guinness. The strain of working with a hostile crew ensured it was the last movie Lucas ever directed.*

with his protagonists. Stone tends to a subjective point of view both with the camera and in his writing. He uses the protagonists to launch the story and often they are in every scene of the movie. 'The most interesting thing in casting is to find an actor when he is about to change, to get him at the point when he's going to make a shift in his personality,' he says. 'Michael Douglas had never been tough before *Wall Street*. Willem Dafoe had always been playing bad guys but he went towards the positive side of the spectrum with *Platoon*. I think that's what's exciting about directing actors, to find something new in them.'

Sydney Pollack started out as an actor and worked as an acting coach in New York before he began to direct. Most actors constantly bitch about directors who don't understand acting and Pollack was no exception. 'Most of my work as an actor was defending myself against stupid directors because most directors

Battle fatigue: Oliver Stone won an Oscar for Platoon *but he's still fighting to make movies his own way.*

I worked with didn't know a damn thing about actors or acting,' he says. 'They understood cameras and lenses and they were full of technique and I hated all of them. And all of the other actors I worked with hated them. We used to talk in the dressing room about what the hell we were going to do with this jerk.' It's a view shared by Barbra Streisand, who worked with Pollack on *The Way We Were*, 'A lot of directors don't know what they want or how to communicate what they want. They deal in results: "Do it faster". But Sydney knows ways to talk to actors that somehow make them feel they're arriving at a new place by themselves. There's a creative way to talk to actors and there's a clumsy way, and Sydney knows the creative way.' Pollack is adept at articulating what he wants in a language that actors can understand. 'I'm orientated always as an actor,' he says. 'That was how I started, and I worked my way into the other aspects of it by using the same principles that I used to use to breakdown and understand and get inside a part. Logic is not what produces behaviour in an actor. What you try to do as a director is find an actor's logic and an actor's logic is all emotional.'

Because movies are shot out of sequence, only the director knows what Pollack calls 'the emotional graph of where the picture has to be'. This has important implications for the relationship between a director and an actor, which is quite different from that which exists between their counterparts in the theatre. According to Pollack, the way he works with actors, who are about to perform for the movie-camera, is quite opposite to the way he would work with actors who are preparing to perform on stage. 'In film, as opposed to theatre, an actor doesn't have to understand at all how they did what they did or why they do what they do. You just have to do it once and the camera has to be rolling.' Pollack tries to stack the odds in his favour by rolling the camera before the actors are ready. The tragedy for him is seeing an actor give him what he wants before he can capture the moment on film. That moment, which in movies, as opposed to the theatre, is the only thing that matters, may never be repeated.

In theatre, the actor is self-sufficient. He or she must perfect the performance with the director's help. Once that has been achieved, most directors are redundant. 'When you rehearse a play,' says Pollack, 'you spend four weeks with one goal in mind – to wean the actor away from you. You want the actor to become completely independent and to understand all the emotional and psychological moves within the character. And at that critical moment when the curtain goes up, you are completely helpless, you cannot do anything. But it's the reverse on film: the only moment that really counts is when the actors are gone, when everyone's gone, when you're alone in the editing room and have to have the raw material you need to put the film together. It's a much more mosaic medium, and in a sense – actors are going to throw stones at me for this – you almost want a more dependent actor.'

In Pollack's view directors get a lot of credit they don't deserve. 'Most of the time, the actor shows up and does it. It's not the director. An awful lot of the time, directing is just knowing when to shut up and stay out of the way.' Pollack's own interest is in character-driven movies, especially love stories. When working with writers he is preoccupied with the motivation of his protagonists. Frequently he creates such depths of dissension between the mismatched lovers that he has to forego the traditional reconciliation which marks most movie romances. Movies like *The Way We Were*, *Absence of Malice*, *Out of Africa* and *Havana* are typical of Pollack's work. They all end on a bitter-sweet note. The kinds of movies Pollack makes, the meaty roles they afford to their leading players, have made him a popular director among stars. Jane Fonda, Meryl Streep, Natalie Wood, Barbra Streisand, Sally Field, Sidney Poitier, Burt Lancaster, Paul Newman, Dustin Hoffman, Al Pacino and Robert Redford have all worked with him at one time or another.

But many directors are wary of stars. They fear that the star might challenge their own authority. Without being star vehicles as such, every one of Pollack's movies has had stars in it. 'And I've never not had control,' he says. 'In most cases, movie stars hire themselves out because they trust and are seduced by the character they want to play. The idea of real luxury to intelligent movie stars – and most of them are intelligent – is to find a director they can trust, so they can bury themselves in the part they are playing.'

Out of the fifteen movies Pollack has made, Robert Redford has appeared in seven of them, most recently in *Havana* where he plays an American gambler who falls in love with a Cuban revolutionary. Speaking of Redford, Pollack says, 'He's become

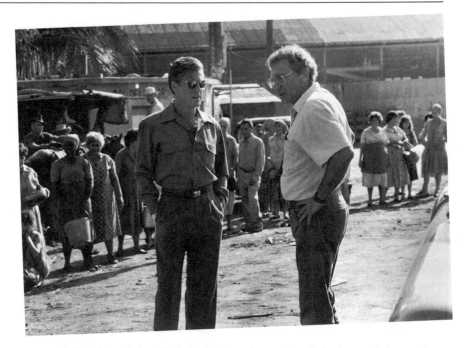

Pollack directs Robert Redford in Havana, *the seventh movie they have worked on together and the most arduous shoot of Pollack's career.*

for me a kind of alter ego in terms of the roles he plays. He has this mixture, if you will, of the shiny exterior, the golden boy, and this very complicated, darker interior, very like America.'

Directors are sometimes susceptible to the aura that some stars project. The first time Martin Scorsese worked with a movie star was when he directed Paul Newman in *The Color of Money*. Scorsese doesn't count De Niro as a star in the same way – they have been working together for too long and know each other too well for that – but Newman was different. 'Newman was a star to me because I was a young boy when I saw him on the screen,' says Scorsese. 'I think Woody Allen talks about this, the pre-twenty-one syndrome. Anybody you saw before the age of twenty-one on the screen, you'd be a little nervous in directing them. After twenty-one it's not a problem for some reason. With Paul Newman, it took me a while to get past the image that I had seen on the screen for so many years.'

The process of moulding an actor's performance continues on into the editing room. There is a special intimacy that exists between an editor and a director. It is similar to the intimacy that the director might enjoy with a writer but it is different because the editing room is the very last stage where all judgements are final. 'Editing is the final rewrite,' says Freeman Davies, who has edited most of director Walter Hill's movies, including *Southern Comfort*, *Streets of Fire* and *Red Heat*. There is a saying in Hollywood that films are never made, they are always re-made, in the cutting room. During production the director has to endure constant frustration. Because the *sturm und drang* of film production

Star-struck: Martin Scorsese directed his boyhood hero, Paul Newman, in The Color of Money.

is so all consuming, it's difficult for a director to keep the movie in perspective while it's being shot. There are too many other demands crowding the director's time and energy – there's just no time for reflection. In the editing room he or she is alone. There's no space between the director and the material. In the editing room, making the movie becomes a direct sculpting process. 'The most fun I have is when I'm in the editing room,' says Steven Spielberg. 'It becomes very personal and rather wonderful. I love that isolation, especially after the cacophony, the sheer white noise of a movie crew on location or on a sound stage. Just the relief from the din is rewarding. Directing is not my happiest time. Directing is very hard. It's very, very hard.'

Most directors never quite know what to expect when they go into the cutting room. According to John Boorman, 'A scene that feels vital in the script sometimes becomes redundant in the editing stage; a complex tracking shot that looked beautiful in the rushes can seem painfully slow or contrived when cut into the film ... A movie grows and develops organically from stage to stage and you never know exactly how it will turn out.' In the editing room, you have to begin again, see the movie anew, and be prepared to sacrifice anything, no matter how precious, to make it work. 'I have one feeling all the way through the making of the film and that is that nothing is sacred,' says Ivan Reitman. 'No matter how hard I've worked, no matter how much money was spent in producing a particular scene, it's not sacred. It doesn't have to stay there. One of the things I love doing after seeing the first rough cut of any film is to go through the movie, scene by scene, with the editing staff and say, "If you could change anything – forget about the fact that we spent weeks shooting a particular scene – if we took it out, would it be better?"'

The first cut is always over-long, sometimes by as much as two hours. It usually tells you whether you have a film or not and for some directors, viewing the first cut can be nerve-racking. Sydney Pollack, who confesses to working more out of anxiety than optimism, dreads the moment. He says that he has never seen a first cut that didn't make him want to commit suicide. But like many directors, Pollack finds the editing process endlessly fascinating. 'It's always better or worse but never exactly as you imagined it,' he says. Nothing is what it seems. 'You have to be like a very good diagnostician when a patient comes to you and says, "My toe is sore". And you look at the toe and there is nothing wrong with the toe. And you start tracking nerves back and pretty soon you find that when he steps down, a nerve gets compressed between two vertebrae in his back, and he's perceiving the pain in his toe. Often you're confronted with this in a film when something in the first ten minutes will make something in the second ten minutes not play.' Pollack says that he never stops learning about editing. Everything that he thought was true, is not necessarily so. All rules are off. 'For example, you begin to see that slower creates the impression of more speed. Countless times I've had a critic at the studio say, "That scene is too long. Can't we cut it?" And I've lengthened it, and they'll say, "Oh, it's much faster now. You must have taken a lot out of it." Things are never what they seem in editing and you must never listen to someone who doesn't understand that process.'

Not everybody respects the privacy of the editing room. If the director's cut of the movie is judged to be unsound, the editor and his equipment, the Steenbeck, may be commandeered by the studio executives. Jim Clark is a veteran British editor who has cut most of John Schlesinger's movies, including *Darling*, *Midnight Cowboy*, *Marathon Man*, *Yanks* and *Honky Tonk Freeway*. Clark recalls that the editing of *Honky Tonk Freeway*, a big-budget comedy which promptly vanished from cinema screens, was especially contentious. 'The cutting room has become the last ditch for saving a picture,' he says. 'The executives are trying to secure their positions, because if the film fails, they'll be moved on. It's like musical chairs and producers get very neurotic. They're on your back long before a film is finished, at rough cut. They're on the director's back too. You get a group of people round the Steenbeck giving their opinions, and the editor has to take a back seat and simply become a mechanic. With *Honky Tonk Freeway*, that was a daily occurrence towards the end. The first version Schlesinger and I put together was the best; after that it was completely mauled.'

For most directors the arduous process of making a movie doesn't really end until the film is released. Although special previews before a sample audience can help a director anticipate how a movie might play to the paying public, and how the movie should be recut accordingly, moviegoers are notoriously unpredictable and no one really knows how they are going to respond to the finished film once it goes into commercial release. Most directors make movies because they want to reach a wide audience so the commercial success of a movie is of intense personal interest to them, beyond the merely pecuniary considerations. 'You always want acclaim of every sort,' says Ivan Reitman. 'First of all you want a lot of people to see your movies. And then you want people to praise your movies. And you want to get nice shiny trophies for your movies.'

For some directors the approval of the critics is as important, if not more so, than the movie's commercial success. It's surprising how sensitive some directors are when it comes to the reviews. Alan Parker, the British-born director who has made a string of commercial movies such as *Midnight Express* and *Fame*, is forever blasting away at the British Press for their failure to appreciate his work. Oliver Stone, who wrote the screenplay for Parker's *Midnight Express*, and won an Oscar for it, is equally despondent. He resents the way critics categorize him as a violent filmmaker who lacks subtlety. 'The only ally I have is the future,' he says. 'I'm looking forward to a younger generation of critics who might view the films that I have made differently.'

Martin Scorsese who, because of the kinds of films he makes, relies on the critics to boost his audiences, maintains that the reviewers in America almost destroyed his career. 'The critics liked *Mean Streets*,' he says. 'They liked *Alice Doesn't Live Here Anymore*. And then the third picture I made was *Taxi Driver*, and they liked that very much. *New York, New York* wasn't received that way and I remember being very depressed about that. I remember taking about two and a half years to get myself back together to make *Raging Bull*. When I did *Raging Bull*, I actually thought that that would be my last picture in America. I thought it was the end. It was well received and it taught me one thing which is to never, never try to do what you think other people want. The idea is to just try to do what you think is right.'

Were Erich von Stroheim alive today, he would be more able to follow Scorsese's dictum – to do what he thinks is right – than he ever could have when he was under the stern tutelage of Irving Thalberg. In a sense, von Stroheim does live on. He has been reincarnated as Francis Coppola or maybe as Michael Cimino. Von Stroheim's ghost, which haunts the old MGM lot – now owned by Columbia Pictures, which is itself owned by the Japanese – is surely amused. Today, directors are more powerful than they have ever been. The time when they were on contract to the studio, and under the supervision of a producer is long gone. That hasn't meant that the quality of movies made in Hollywood has improved. But it does mean the producers of the studio era have seen their bright chimpanzees turn into gorillas. Now producers have to fight, plead, flatter, cajole and beg to get their way. Thalberg must be spinning in his grave.

CHAPTER SIX

FIRE-FIGHTERS AND
FORTUNE-HUNTERS

The producer is an authoritarian figure who risks nothing, presumes to know public taste, and always wants to change the end of a film.
Federico Fellini, director

The way I see it, my function is to be responsible for everything.
David O. Selznick, producer

One day a screenwriter, Joseph L. Mankiewicz, went to see his boss, Louis B. Mayer. 'I want to write and direct,' said Mankiewicz. 'No!' Mayer shouted back, 'You have to produce *first*. You have to *crawl* before you can walk.' Which, thought Mankiewicz, was as good a definition of producing as he'd ever heard. Producers have been getting a lousy press ever since: they are the fat cats, who can be seen each May at the Cannes Film Festival sunning themselves on the terrace of the Carlton Hotel, their sweaty paunches, speckled with cigar ash, straining the buttons of their shirts, a giant, gold medallion glinting through the luxuriant tufts of their chest hair, a bored starlet dangling from each elbow. They are fast-talking hustlers, brash, flashy liars who have neither money nor talent but excel at exploiting those who have either or both. In short, movie producers have an image problem.

That much was clear as early as 1937 when David O. Selznick, the legendary producer of *Gone With the Wind*, admitted that 'of all the people who come to Hollywood, I have yet to have a person come to me and say, "I am anxious to be a producer". They want to write, direct, be cameramen or actors – mostly actors – but for some mysterious reason they don't want to be producers ...' Selznick was puzzled by this because in an age when producers were far more powerful than stars or directors, he was the greatest producer of his generation. 'The difference between myself and other producers,' he once said, 'is I am interested in the thousands and thousands of details that go into the making of a film. It is the sum total of all these things that either makes a picture or destroys it.' The way Selznick saw it, his function was to be responsible for everything. He believed that a producer, in order to be able to produce properly, 'must be able, if necessary, to sit down and write the scene, and if he is criticizing a director, he must be able – not merely to say "I don't like it", but tell him how he would direct it himself. He must be able to go into a cutting room, and if he doesn't like the cutting of the sequence, which is more often true than not, he must be able to recut the sequence.'

At the same time as he is paying attention to the smallest details, the producer needs to be able to retain perspective on the movie. Selznick was dubious about the ability of even the best directors to keep a proper distance. 'The great danger in a producing set-up is that the director, being close to the picture, on the set day-by-day and in the cutting room day-by-day, has no perspective on the picture as a whole, on its story values, entertainment values, or, least of all, its commercial values.' And he had little time for those directors who insisted on producing the movies they directed. According to Selznick, 'Ninety-nine directors out of a hundred are worthless as producers, particularly for themselves'.

We know so much about the everyday details of Selznick's working life because he was a fanatical memo-writer. To the consternation of his secretarial staff, Selznick loved nothing better than to dictate lengthy memos late into the night, and often on into the next morning, detailing his thoughts on whatever script, casting, make-up, production or marketing problems were foremost in his mind at the time. His memos on *Gone With the Wind* are an exhaustive lesson in the scope and depth of a producer's responsibilities. They cover a multitude of details: the purchase price to the rights of Margaret Mitchell's novel (Selznick paid $50 000, then the largest price ever paid for a book); the hiring of Sidney Howard to write the screenplay; the hiring of Oliver Garrett, F. Scott Fitzgerald and Ben Hecht to do rewrites; endless comments on their various drafts; the casting of Scarlett O'Hara, Rhett Butler and the other leads; the possibility of making two separate movies from the book; the distribution of the film through MGM (which was the only way Selznick could secure the services of Clark Gable, who was under contract to Mayer); the dismissal of George Cukor as director and the hiring of Victor Fleming; the hiring of Sam Wood to replace Fleming when he fell ill with exhaustion; the use of Technicolor film stock; Clark Gable's accent; Clark Gable's costume; the score; the inclusion of Rhett Butler's immortal punch line, 'Frankly, my dear, I don't give a damn', which the censor wished to omit; the credits; the essential need for an intermission; the invitation list for the premiere in Altanta; the price of theatre tickets ($1.50 for preferred seats); the possibility of making a sequel.

At the same time as Selznick was firing off memos on *Gone With the Wind*, he was sending precise instructions to Alfred Hitchcock concerning the direction of *Rebecca*. Hitchcock's first treatment prompted a blistering response from Selznick who, never one to hold back, claimed he was distressed, shocked and 'disappointed beyond words', by the way in which the novel had been desecrated. Subsequent memos to Hitchcock addressed a succession of topics: the speed of production – Hitch was far too slow for Selznick's

The producer as auteur: *David O. Selznick sent Alfred Hitchcock detailed suggestions about how to direct* Rebecca, *many of which Hitchcock actually followed.*

taste; the opening sequence – Selznick thought it was worthless because it lacked mood; the direction of Joan Fontaine and Laurence Olivier – Selznick wanted Olivier to speed up his delivery. Hitchcock joked that he never had time to read Selznick's memos but the fact that Selznick's suggestions were invariably followed to the letter indicates otherwise. When Selznick said that 'great films, successful films, are made in their *every detail* according to the vision of one man', he was not referring to the director.

Although Selznick was exceptional, most producers enjoyed

authority over the director during the thirties and forties. It was the producer who supervised the writing of the screenplay, often bringing in a director just before the start of production. Once filming had been completed, it was routine for the director to go on to another picture, leaving the producer to supervise the editing of the footage. With the collapse of the studio system, the producers' power diminished. The change in their status is aptly described by Pandro S. Berman, who produced the Astaire-Rogers musicals at RKO before moving on to MGM. 'My greatest contribution was to find the story material, develop it into a screenplay, cast it, and make the picture, usually using other studio personnel for all these jobs. To make a distinction between the producer I am describing and the producer of today, the producer of today is more of an agent, a packager, a promoter, or a financial man who will put things together and take them to a studio, a distribution company, or a bank and get financing. That method has had a very great effect in that the producer has abdicated his function as the creative man in the set-up. He has gone to other business activities, leaving the director as the creative influence.' Today, lamented Berman, 'the director is the boss.'

David O. Selznick was mystified as to why so few people aspired to be producers. He couldn't understand why the job at which he excelled appeared to be so lacking in esteem. Matters have not improved since then. Producers still have an image problem today although the explanation for that is actually not so very mysterious. One reason is that some producers really are exactly as the public imagines them to be. They really are brash and flashy and about as trustworthy as Goebbels, and they really do tend to tow a shoal of bimbos in their wake. But these producers, who embody the stereotype, are a minority. They are the low end of the market. They are the insect world of movieland's animal kingdom. Even though most producers aren't like that, they still have to share the same image problem for the simple reason that most of us are completely mystified as to what it is that producers actually do. It's not an easy question to answer because one characteristic that producers do share with the insect world is that there are so many different species of them. Besides the common producer, there are executive producers, associate producers, line producers, supervising producers, production supervisors, co-producers, production executives, executives in charge of the production ... And the definition of any one of these titles can change from movie to movie.

For example, in a wonderful instance of producer overload, the final credits for director Terry Gilliam's movie, *The Adventures of Baron Munchausen*, solemnly acknowledged every one of the varieties listed above. *Munchausen* is something of an extreme example because the costs of the movie went wildly out of control and, as the budget burgeoned, the financiers and insurers scrambled to protect their investment by appointing more and more producers to supervise the shooting. 'Suddenly it became like a train out of control,' Thomas Schühly, the original producer, said at the time. 'It went faster and faster until you couldn't stop it anymore.' The budget blossomed from $23.5 million to more than $40 million. Money ran out after the seventh week of filming at which point the financiers suspended production for two weeks and threatened to dismiss the director and the producer unless they agreed to make drastic cuts. Gilliam tore out 44 pages from the 126-page screenplay and filming resumed. 'The problem with a film, once it's gone out of control, once the basic structure and plan for the making of the film has gone, is that you can't stop it,' says Gilliam. 'This hurtling juggernaut's going for the precipice and you keep extending the precipice. Basically, you're building out as fast as the thing's moving, and eventually the structure collapses and falls into the abyss.' The problems of making *Munchausen* were compounded by the fact that Gilliam promptly fell out with Schühly, and the two of them stopped talking to each other just before the start of principal photography; not a promising start for any movie. 'Had the production been properly controlled from the beginning,' says Gilliam, 'half of these people wouldn't have been needed.' Of course, it's quite impossible to determine who did what on *Munchausen* without obtaining a glossary from one of the few people who would be in a position to give you such a thing. So, for the record, Gilliam's explanation is as follows.

The 'executive producer' raised the cash to make the movie, a process in which the 'producer' and the director also participated. (Frequently, the executive producer title is given to the head of the company that finances the movie.) The 'line producer' dealt with the day-to-day business of making the movie. 'He really does the work,' says Gilliam. The 'co-producer' was a friend of Gilliam's who had been involved in the movie from an early stage and who, according to Gilliam, acted as an intermediary between the director and the producer 'when things turned nasty'. The 'executive in charge of production' was another line producer, who left before shooting was completed but retained a credit nevertheless. The 'production supervisor' was the Italian line producer, who was necessary because *Munchausen* was shot with an Italian crew at the Cinecittà studio complex in Rome. The 'supervising producer' – a term borrowed from television terminology when there are too many producers and a new title is needed – was appointed to take over the production by the completion guarantor. This is a financing company which guarantees to fund the completion of the movie should anything go amiss during production, which in the case of *Munchausen* turned out to be something of an understatement. The 'production executive' was appointed by Lloyds of London to supervise the post-production of the movie. And as for the 'producer', what did he do? That depends on who you speak to, but for the purposes of general definition the job of the producer is to avoid the kind of problems that occurred far too frequently on *The Adventures of Baron Munchausen*. As they say in Hollywood, the producer's job is to 'put out fires'.

Even so, it's tricky to define exactly what it is that a producer does because a producer can do almost anything or almost nothing to deserve the actual credit of 'producer'. The amorphous qualifications that are required for the role are aptly summed up by the writer, director and comic, Carl Reiner: 'I didn't realize, even though I had been in the business for so long, that anybody who has taste is a producer. That is all you have to have, with a little bit of ability. If you can be a producer without taste, you have to have money. You have to have one or the other. Also, it is nice to have some kind of heft. You can also have a piece of property. That will give you heft. You can say, "I just bought all of Joseph Conrad's manuscripts, all of the unpublished ones". That will give you heft until they say, "Who is Joseph Conrad?" That's when you've got no heft. But many things can give you heft. One successful production will give you heft. An attitude will give you heft. Also, you can have heft if you are a very smart guy, who knows what you are doing.'

In fact, it requires no qualifications whatever to call yourself a producer. But it requires enormous intelligence, charm, patience, perseverance, physical stamina, guts and a shrewd gambler's instinct to do it well. On the one hand, there is no producer's union you have to join before you can legitimately claim the title. You don't need to have ever made a movie, or even worked on a movie in any capacity. Anyone can take the title of 'producer' and many, who neither have nor desire actual production experience, do so. Producers are frequently drawn from the ranks of ex-agents, displaced studio executives, directors, actors, writers, accountants, managers, lawyers and the sons and daughters-in-law of any of the above. Nepotism still reigns in Hollywood and people can acquire titles thanks to their connections. A great deal of power comes from the elements that are attached to a project, and there are many agents, lawyers, business managers and so on, who get a variant of the producer credit on movies because they control the stars who are attached to the film. For example, the title of 'associate producer' is frequently used as a kind of catch-all credit for, say, the girlfriend or the agent of the star. Consequently it's a moniker that inspires immediate distrust. On the other hand, it's difficult to pull it off for long as a producer if what you are is a fake.

'The producer – if he really is a producer – usually works on a picture longer than anyone else,' says Robert Evans, who has produced such movies as *Chinatown*, *Marathon Man* and *Urban Cowboy*. The producer can be the first one on a movie and the last one off. 'I don't think I really finish this project until it's in a videocassette box somewhere,' says Loretha Jones, who has just produced her first movie, a musical drama called *The Five Heartbeats*. At his or her most involved, the producer conceives the idea for the movie. Maybe it's an article in a newspaper which looks like a promising premise for a story. David Puttnam, the British producer of *Chariots of Fire*, read a feature in the *New York Times Magazine* which he bought as the first step towards what became the movie, *The Killing Fields*.

Producers often have several ideas in development at the same time because the chances of any one idea surviving long enough to make it to the screen are slim. Don Simpson and Jerry Bruckheimer are two of the most successful producers in Hollywood. Their movies include *Flashdance*, *Beverly Hills Cop I and II*, *Top Gun* and *Days of Thunder*. They tend to have as many as twenty ideas in development at any one time, and they estimate that around one

Among the films that have made Robert Evans's career have been Chinatown, Urban Cowboy, *and* Marathon Man *(here, with Dustin Hoffman and Marthe Keller).*

out of six has a chance of making it through to production. And that might not happen for five, six, seven years or more. For example, the seed for what became *Beverly Hills Cop* was planted in Simpson's mind when he was stopped by the Beverly Hills police just because he looked scruffy. It was to be another eight years before the movie was made. Sydney Pollack, who often produces the movies he directs, worked on successive drafts of a screenplay for *Havana* for fourteen years before he finally went into production.

Ideas are sickly things. The mortality rate is high and they need careful nurturing. It can take years for an idea to grow up and there are many pitfalls along the way. Supporting an idea is as expensive as bringing up a child. And like errant kids, they sometimes try to run away from home. Usually when a producer buys the rights to a magazine article or a novel, what he is actually doing is paying for an option which he must renew maybe once a year. The option is usually in the form of a down-payment. If the producer can raise the cash to make the movie, he is then obliged to pay a further sum of money to the person who owns the rights. If he fails to renew the option or it expires, he might lose the idea to another producer. Most screenplays go through several drafts. Each of those rewrites costs money and some producers just can't keep up the payments. This may mean having to sell the screenplay to cover costs and so losing control of their baby. In that case, the producer just has to step back and watch helplessly as the cute little kid upon whom so much effort has been lavished over the years is transformed into a juvenile delinquent in order to cater to someone else's idea of what the public wants to see.

After buying the rights to the idea, in whatever form it might be, the next step is to hire a writer, maybe several writers, and develop the idea into a screenplay. Hiring a writer is the first of many casting decisions the producer must make and it is one of the most crucial. Finding the right writer for the right material is fundamental. And just as the hiring of the writer is the first of many casting decisions, working with the writer is the first of a series of collaborative relationships the producer must negotiate with skill and tact. Briefing the writer and guiding the screenplay so that it develops in the best possible direction means the producer must know what he wants and he must be able to communicate that to the writer in a way that will produce results.

Getting the screenplay into shape is often the most difficult and time-consuming aspect of making a movie. Everything depends on it. 'He or she who has the script is king,' says Don Simpson. 'It's very simple. It doesn't matter whether you're an agent, an actor, a director, a producer or a studio person. If you've got the document that people want to make, you're running the show. It's always about what's on paper.' Different producers approach the process in different ways. Don Simpson likes to test his ideas by pitching them to his partner, Jerry Bruckheimer. Bruckheimer feeds in his own thoughts and together they thrash out a scenario. Then they bring in their development people – all successful producers have an entourage of such people, who are paid to come up with ideas and coax them into screenplays. Hollywood is still a male-dominated world but development is one area in which women, commonly known as 'D-girls', predominate. As a result of a 'development meeting' – when they're not actually making movies, producers like to give the impression they are busy 'taking development meetings' at breakfast, lunch, dinner and all hours in-between – they'll hire a writer, maybe more than one.

Of course, optioning the idea and paying a writer costs money and most producers are firm believers in the theory of OPM – that is, using Other People's Money to finance the development of their ideas. Although the term, 'independent producer' is routinely used to describe producers in Hollywood, it is a misnomer. Few producers are independent in any real sense of the word; they do not fund their activities out of their own pockets. Instead they depend on funding from a financier, usually a studio. They are dependent producers.

One way in which studio bosses put together their production slates is to sign producers to short-term production contracts. These fall under different categories. There are 'first look' deals, by which the producer agrees to give the studio the first opportunity to accept or reject a project before it is submitted to any other studio. In return the studio covers the overheads and pays the producer a fee in advance of making the movie. Another kind of arrangement is the 'exclusive' deal, which commits the producer to developing and producing all his or her projects for one studio. And then there is the 'housekeeping' deal, in which case the producer is given an office on the lot but is otherwise left to fend for him or herself.

Don Simpson and Jerry Bruckheimer signed a deal with Paramount Pictures which doesn't really fall under any of these categories. The studio agreed to supply the cash – some $300 million – to fund the development, production, distribution and marketing of five movies which Simpson and Bruckheimer were committed to produce over five years. Normally, studios insist on the right to approve the script, cast and budget of any movie they finance. In this case, Paramount chose to waive those rights. 'They put up the money, we put up the talent and we meet at the theatre,' said Simpson when the deal was announced. 'We really don't have to talk to anybody or ask anybody's permission about any element. We certainly rely heavily on Paramount's expertise to distribute and market the picture but when it comes to conceiving the movie and making the movie, that's our game totally and solely.'

In the event, what *Variety* describes with characteristic colour as a 'super-producer megadeal', lasted a mere ten months before both parties opted to end their relationship. For the studio, the terms were just too rich to live with. But though the deal eventually imploded under the weight of its own excessive generosity, at the time of its announcement it was hailed as marking a new pinnacle of producer power. It reflected the frenzied competition among studios to secure the services of a handful of high-profile producers.

The entry of the Japanese into Hollywood had upped the ante in this particular game. When Lawrence Gordon, the producer of such hits as *48 Hours* and *Die Hard*, went into partnership with the Japanese electronics company, JVC/Victor, to launch a new production company – he calls it a mini-studio – with a $100-million fund supplied by the Japanese, it was seen as signalling a resurgence of producer power. Then Sony made their famous deal with Jon Peters and Peter Guber to entice them to leave Warners for Columbia. It was in response to these events that Paramount agreed to give Simpson and Bruckheimer such leeway. The producers' previous deal with the studio was coming up for renewal and Paramount knew they would have to give them something special to keep them on the studio lot.

But few producers enjoy such opportunities even if those opportunities may be short-lived, and because they are, in effect, dependent producers they must at some point persuade someone to finance the development of what is, after all, just a bright idea which doesn't as yet exist in any tangible form. He or she must 'pitch' the idea to a potential buyer who will cover the development costs in return for a share of the profits. Making the pitch is at the heart of what a producer does. In fact, it might even be said to be at the heart of what Hollywood is. According to Bernie Brillstein, a producer and manager, who has represented John Belushi and Dan Aykroyd and who was the executive producer of *Ghostbusters*, 'If you're a producer, manager, lawyer, agent, you're the same guy. It's all the same job. You make the pitch.'

The pitch is usually in the form of a meeting between a seller – a producer or a writer or both if, as is quite likely, they work as a team – and a buyer, who is likely to be a studio executive. Producer Lynda Obst became something of an authority on pitching when she wrote a tongue-in-cheek article called 'The Ontology of the Pitch' for *California Magazine*. 'Classically, producers "wind up", that is, prep the group for the right mood, and intrigue them with the "area". The writers do the "pitch" – the actual telling of the story. Producers should try to navigate the meeting for the writers – save it from dangerous twists and deviations from their mutual intentions. They cannot wrest control completely, though, as the real control is always with the buyer – on the other side of the table.' The agenda of a pitch meeting follows a standard routine: small talk, story and 'elements'. 'Elements' is Hollywoodese for big name talent. If the producer can present the idea as a package – with a lead actor, preferably a star, and a director, preferably a known name, then the chances of success are multiplied ten-fold. If the idea has to stand on its own without the benefit of any elements, then the meeting is liable to develop into a wish-fulfilment exercise that is invariably futile and potentially lethal to the project's chances of success. 'Under no circumstances ever allow a pitch to hinge on the casting of one particular person,' counsels Obst. 'This is the easiest route to a pass.' 'Passing on a project' is studiospeak for saying, 'No.' Just as, 'Let me talk to my people', either means the executive doesn't have the authority to make a commitment, or can't decide. Studio executives are forever haunted by the fear that a project they have passed on, will make a fortune for another studio. The easiest way to protect themselves is to sit tight and keep the hapless producer dangling in limbo.

There's no guaranteed method or technique for pitching but Hollywood is rife with rules which are said to increase the odds in your favour. Cardinal Rule Number One: Know your buyer. The whole question of whether the meeting will result in a deal or a pass inevitably comes down to a matter of personal taste so producers try to tailor the presentation of their ideas to the predilections of the individual executive. The most popular technique is to introduce the story by describing it as a hybrid of a pair of hit movies, such as *Ghostbusters* meets *Pretty Woman*, or *Total Recall* meets *Driving*

Miss Daisy. Knowing your buyer also means anticipating what queries are likely to come up after the pitch has been made. According to Lynda Obst, 'You can count on arguing about motivation, because unbeknownst to you, all members of the pitch meeting are closet psychoanalysts. Each of these experts will dazzle you with his ability to debate the fine points of any motivation, venal or otherwise ... You must allow the geniuses to flex their intellectual muscle here because it's through this process that they begin to possess the idea as their own, and thus want to buy it.'

Cardinal Rule Number Two: Keep it short. Firstly, these people have brief attention spans. Secondly, if they forget what you tell them, then you've wasted your time. Remember that if you are pitching to a junior executive, he or she will have to repeat the substance of what you say to the boss. Many pitches which are well received at a junior level subsequently disappear within a game of Chinese whispers. Consequently, pitches tend to be based on plot, not character. They are designed to accommodate ideas which are high-concept. 'Think of it as the *Reader's Digest* condensed-novel version of the screenplay,' says Obst. It's for this reason that good pitches often make lousy screenplays. That's why some executives, such as Universal's, Tom Pollock, are loath to take pitch meetings. 'I think the pitch as an art form is overrated,' he says.

Cardinal Rule Number Three: Pitch to someone who can say, 'Yes'. The level of the executive to whom you pitch is crucial because at any given studio there are dozens of production and development executives who have no authority to make a decision without referring it up to their boss. This can be devastating because rather than admit to their lack of stature, a studio executive is likely to keep you on hold forever. In fact, there are only two people who matter, the president of production and the studio boss. Producers who have any kind of muscle will only pitch to one of the top cats. Ned Tanen, Tom Pollock's predecessor at

Universal who subsequently moved on to run Paramount, has heard more pitches than he cares to remember. He has this advice for the pitcher who is lucky enough to find himself before a studio boss. 'Know your subject. Be specific, be succinct, don't ramble all over the room. Don't try to sell more than one thing. You are not selling vacuum cleaners. Be passionate about what you are doing without being foolish, and try to act like an adult.'

The problem for the studio boss is to try to anticipate how the public will respond to the idea when it is eventually released as a movie, which is likely to be some two years later. So the producer needs to stimulate the boss's gastric juices by pitching the advertising campaign for the movie at the same time as he or she is pitching the storyline. 'You have to come to your pitch with great enthusiasm,' says Lynda Obst. 'You have to be infused with the notion that your idea is the greatest idea of all time, and you have to have what we call a one-sheet, which is the poster for the movie, in your mind. You have to be able to sell the poster for the movie. You do your best to create a carnival, party-like atmosphere. You have to make this person feel that being in the room with you is the only place to be on this Tuesday afternoon in Hollywood. You drop names. You let people know that this idea has been overheard at important restaurants by significant people. You give the impression that the phone's been ringing off the hook. You have to make the buyer of your script believe, before they've even heard the idea, that you are the person that they have to be in business with. And then you start talking fast.'

'People do it all different ways,' says Brian Grazer, who is in partnership with director Ron Howard in the successful production company, Imagine Entertainment. Grazer has produced such hits as the Tom Hanks mermaid movie, *Splash*, and *Parenthood*. A small, wiry, hyperkinetic man, Grazer was born to pitch. 'When I think of ideas for movies, I view the world as one thing or the other,' he says. 'It's either black or white. It's really clear to me.' Grazer is a professional enthusiast. He talks faster than most people can think. In fact he speaks at such a high velocity that he has difficulty sustaining a conversation, which is invariably in the form of a monologue, for much more than fifteen minutes. If you wanted to learn the art of the pitch from a true master, Grazer would be your man. Grazer's technique is to pretend he is a junior editor for *60 Minutes*, a fast-paced news show, and that he only has two seconds to catch the interest of Mike Wallace, the front man. 'So what I try to do is hit him with the headlines of the idea. Usually my departure point is a question – "What would you do if this happened to you?" And then I go on for maybe twenty-five sentences and I try to engage my audience in an exchange so that I can use their imagination along with my imagination to further the idea. That method will succeed at the level of 95 per cent.' But don't ask for your money back. Any advice on pitching is non-refundable.

Pitches either result in a pass – go away and try somewhere else – or a 'green light', which means the studio agrees to fund the next stage, whether it be the writing of a screenplay or the putting of a finished screenplay into production. Frequently, the result of a pitch is inconclusive. The studio might express serious interest in proceeding further but only if, say, Arnold Schwarzenegger is prepared to play the role of the Wicked Witch of the North, or Sydney Pollack agrees to direct, or you can cut the budget by half. In those instances, a producer finds him or herself faced not with a pass, nor with a green light exactly, but with a flashing amber. These moments are trying on the nerves and living through them is what a producer's life is all about.

In order to get a green light, producers practise a subtle form of psychological warfare. They try to create a climate of opinion around a project by leaking titbits about what they are doing round town. The ideal forum for spreading good word-of-mouth is over breakfast, lunch or dinner. The speed with which gossip travels in Hollywood is extraordinary and lunch's whispered rumour can be universal wisdom by breakfast the next morning. Like impatient motorists who rev up their engines while waiting for the lights to change, producers stuck on amber want to let everyone know they're around. More often than not, if you're on amber for too long, the lights may change back to red. The studio might go cold on the idea or a new management might arrive and put all the projects which have been developed by the previous regime into 'turnaround'. That means they are frozen and put up for sale to anyone who wants to pay off the costs that have been incurred on the projects thus far.

Projects can go into turnaround at any time. Lynda Obst was all set to make a movie for Columbia called *Skirts*. Five weeks before the start of principal photography, the studio pulled the plug when David Puttnam left and Dawn Steel stepped in to replace him. 'The worst thing about it was, I was crewed up, I had a full staff, and I had to call forty people and tell them that they weren't working through Christmas and that they had to find another job,' says Obst. 'But I do believe that any studio head or any new administration has the right to re-examine what they are about to spend a lot of money on. In fact they would be fiscally irresponsible if they didn't do it. That's how disasters occur, when you actually go ahead and make a movie that you don't want to release. We could have spent ten months working on that film, and if this administration didn't like the film that had been made, they would have dumped it. And I would rather have a film aborted so it can come back together at another studio where they want to make it, than go ahead and do all of that work and have it lost forever on the shelf.'

Having a project go into turnaround is not necessarily a disaster. Lynda Obst and her partner, Debra Hill, had an exclusive deal at

Disney. The two producers came across a screenplay called *The Fisher King* and they persuaded Disney to buy the rights. But then the studio got cold feet – the story was darkly satirical – and put the project into turnaround. By that time, Obst had moved on – she had a 'first look' deal at Columbia and thanks to the enthusiasm of an executive there, the studio picked up the rights.

The next step for a producer is to find a director and cast the lead players. Enter the agents. 'We can't make pictures without them,' says Obst. 'The perfect film is a function of reality, not just idealism. That is to say, "Who's available?"' Obst and Hill sat down with some agencies and combed through their lists of available directors. Eventually, at Creative Artists Agency, the name of Terry Gilliam came up. Obst and Hill knew that Gilliam's name was guaranteed to inspire fear and trembling in the hearts of many studio executives, especially those at Columbia, which was the studio that lost a fortune on *The Adventures of Baron Munchausen*. The most expensive European movie ever made, *Munchausen* was a legendary disaster. Obst admits when they first mentioned Gilliam's name at the studio, 'there was a bit of bracing, sort of hands-on-chairs and white knuckles'. It was a risk but after meeting Gilliam in London, Obst and Hill were convinced he was right for the job and that he could work within a budget. After *Munchausen*, says Hill, Gilliam wanted to be 'redeemed from his past. He wants to come in on budget, and he wants to create a mainstream Hollywood movie.' Gilliam's explanation for the *Munchausen* debacle is that it was caused by the fact that he did not have a strong producer to restrain his natural excesses and act as a buffer. According to Gilliam, a producer is there 'to protect me and keep me away from all the political machinations of the studio. That's the first thing. And the other thing is to keep me in line, somebody who says, "If you are going to do that, it's going to cost this". Once I know that, I can then start prioritizing things. But if nobody tells me, "No", I will just keep going and going. My imagination will keep writing. They have to give me parameters all the time, otherwise I don't know where to stop.'

Together with Gilliam, Obst and Hill secured the agreement of Jeff Bridges and Robin Williams to take the lead roles. Obst admits that signing Williams was a significant step towards making *The Fisher King* a reality. 'It's very important to have a star of Robin's calibre in this movie for a couple of reasons. First of all, the studio's commitment to marketing the movie in a large-scale way is dependent on some element that they can guarantee will help open the movie. [With Robin's participation] it becomes a major motion picture. It gets a major slot for release. Issues that concern Debra and I, like the budget and the schedule, start to become reasonable. I don't know that this picture would have been made at this studio without a major star. We needed an actor that a studio would commit this amount of money to, and that's what Robin secured for us. And in many cases, in this case actually, it delivered us our green light.'

In a sense, movies are made before the camera starts to turn. When David Mamet was preparing to direct his first movie, *House of Games*, he was fortunate enough to have a veteran producer at his side. Mike Hausman, who among many other movies produced *Amadeus*, had a favourite axiom: All mistakes are made in pre-production. Once the cameras start turning, it's very difficult to keep a movie under control if the planning and preparation work is sloppy. 'The most important place in the world to get your production under control is during the preparation process,' says ex-Columbia boss turned producer, Dawn Steel. 'You have to be extraordinarily well-prepared. Once you've started shooting, there's very little in my opinion that you can do to stop an out of control movie.'

One of the most important things a producer does before filming can begin is to hire the crew. The decision of who's going to be your art director, who's going to be your cinematographer, and who's going to be your costume designer are critically important creative decisions. And all these decisions have an impact on the budget. 'The budget is subject to change up until the day you start to shoot,' says Hill. 'It's all a matter of layering things. You do a script breakdown. You breakdown your locations versus your studio work. The costume designer adds something. The production designer adds something. Each creative person you bring in adds something new.' And more than anyone, Gilliam is prone to add something new. That's just the way he works. 'I intended at the beginning not to do anything,' he says of *The Fisher King*. 'I was going to make a little film. I was going to make a Woody Allen-style film. People just walking down the streets. Well unfortunately I've discovered I can't do that. The thing starts growing.'

Securing the studio's agreement to a budget figure is the stage at which many movies founder. Budgets are divided into above-the-line and below-the-line costs. Above-the-line means the costs incurred by the creative participants – principally, the fees for the stars, the director, the writer and the producers. The below-the-line figure covers everything else – the physical costs of making the movie. Studios decide how much they want to spend per picture depending in part on who's in that picture and how marketable the movie will be. They make a guess as to the likely box-office earnings and they arrive at a below-the-line figure that makes sense in the light of that. Inevitably, the studio wants to spend less than the producers think they need and the weeks leading up to, and often beyond the start of principal photography, are fraught with continual give and take. Eventually a budget of $23 million was agreed for *The Fisher King* – $13 million of which was above-the-line, and $10 million below-the-line.

Once filming begins, the producer's role changes dramatically.

Once the cameras roll, the director is in charge. 'There is a moment when the director takes it over,' says Albert S. Ruddy, the producer of *The Godfather*. 'And that is why you've got to hire the right director.' If the director and the producer do not see eye-to-eye then you're in trouble. No producer and no studio executive can force an intransigent director to do something unless he wants to do it. Directors know that studios are loath to abort a shoot. During the production of *Heaven's Gate*, the director Michael Cimino knew that the more money the studio, United artists, had riding on the movie, the less likely they were to pull out. Cimino played a shrewd game of poker with the UA's production executives. Even as the costs of making the movie were spiralling out of control, he gave them just enough encouragement to forestall abandoning the movie. Every now and again, Cimino would summon the joint production chiefs, Steven Bach and David Field, to join him on location in Montana and view an assembly of the latest footage. Each time Bach and Field went out on location fully resolved to bring their director to heel, and each time they returned, chastened by his artistry. In other words, they blinked. 'When you're talking about an important director – and a director whose personal vision is that important to the film – you have only two options,' said Bach at the time. 'One is to continue and control the production as tightly as you can, and the other is to pull the plug. David [Field] and I deplored the extent to which the picture was going over budget, but at the same time we were awed and incredibly proud of what was coming out of the camera.' Or, as Cecil B. De Mille once said, 'What do you want me to do, stop shooting and release it as *The Five Commandments*?'

Confrontations are inevitable. Loretha Jones says that 'the toughest part of her job is when she has to have a confrontation with her director Robert Townsend. Jones had to work hard to keep the costs of making *The Five Heartbeats* within its relatively

'*What do you want me to do, stop shooting and release it as* The Five Commandments?'
Cecil B. De Mille on set.

modest $9 million budget and that sometimes meant saying, 'No',
to her director. 'The part of my job I like the least is when I have
to talk to him about deleting something from the script that is
creatively important just for economic reasons. They're like his
children, you know. It's like coming to someone and saying, "I'm
sorry, but we're going to have to amputate your child's hand
because we don't have enough money to buy a second glove."'
But compromise, not control, is the name of the game. 'I don't
think you ever actually control the director,' says Lynda Obst.
'The whole notion of controlling a director is some studio fiction.

The fact of the matter is that no one controls anyone in real life. You manage people, you manage crises and you avert them. But if you actually try to control a director, you'll squeeze his vision out of the tube. You can't take a terrifically gifted director and control him, or he wouldn't be a terrifically gifted director.' Hill agrees, 'It's a collaboration and it's a compromise. If you want a sunny scene and it rains, you shoot it in the rain. If you can't get the actor you want, you shoot it with a different actor. Everything is compromise. That's what filmmaking is.'

During production the director is under enormous strain and it's the producer's job to protect the director. 'My primary obligation is to the film. I want to make sure that the director's vision of it is protected,' says Loretha Jones. According to Albert S. Ruddy, the producer of *The Godfather*, 'You must build a wall around [the director] so that he can address the greatest possible amount of his creative energies to the execution of the film and not be concerned with a lot of the other pressures.' One purpose for building that wall is to keep the studio off the director's back. Not only do studio executives get nervous once filming starts, but many of them are frustrated filmmakers, and sometimes they can't resist turning up on set and getting in the way. 'I call the studio before they call me,' says Loretha Jones. 'I pick the times that I invite them to the set. It's a matter of making them feel involved without letting them interfere. It's a delicate balance.'

During production the producer's activities depend on events. 'There really isn't a routine,' says Debra Hill. 'Sometimes it's going to the office and signing cheques and doing production reports and cost reports. Sometimes it's going to the editing room to make sure a certain scene is being cut properly. Most of the time it's standing around putting out fires. Most of the time it's crisis management.' The producer depends heavily on the line producer and the production manager to alert him or her to impending catastrophes. Dennis Jones is a veteran line producer. 'It's essential to be conscious of rumblings that go on in the crew,' he says. It's vital to correct any slippage early on because the costs of making a film can easily multiply. According to Ruddy, 'You have the various departments – camera, sound, wardrobe – and if you lose, or start sliding, in one department it affects every other department. If the set you've constructed is not staying up, then you can't proceed with set dressing; and everybody else is not working, literally, but is being paid nevertheless.'

The danger signs usually manifest themselves early on. The first two or three weeks are crucial. At that stage, if production is falling, say a day behind each week, that can mean that over the duration of a ten-week shoot the schedule will slip back by two weeks. With crew costs running at around $60 000 a day that adds up to an additional $600 000. Once you start to factor in the costs of keeping the stars beyond their agreed contract periods the figures soon mushroom. One expedient is to cut scenes from the script. According to Dennis Jones, 'Most scripts are usually too long when you go into the film. The director wants to have a film from which he can withdraw scenes which don't work and you never can tell when you start the film. If you cut them out too soon, then you may be cutting out scenes which would have worked. So it's a delicate balance. You have to be concerned to protect the film at the same time as trying to control the costs.'

During the first weeks of *The Fisher King* shoot on location in New York, the schedule began to slip. The main problems sprang from the unseasonal rain and the fact that New York is a notoriously difficult city for filmmakers. But Gilliam's tendency to come up with elaborate ideas with no advance notice strained resources further. According to production manager, Tony Marks, 'You're dealing with a volcanic imagination and what you're trying to do is provide the tools for the volcanic imagination to be realized on the screen. It ain't easy.' Debra Hill was unfazed. 'We've been doing a lot of thinking since we've fallen behind and I think the word of the day is simplify,' she says. 'I don't really think it's necessary to cut scenes in order to get back on schedule. I think we just have to simplify what we've planned.' In the event, the production ended up being over-schedule by nine days and over-budget by around $1.5 million – that is over-schedule, over-budget but by no means out of control.

The producer's responsibilities do not end with the delivery of the finished movie. Although it might seem logical to assume that a studio which has invested several million dollars in a movie will automatically market it as well as it possibly can, this is often not the case. The costs of releasing a movie to cinemas around the country are substantial and it is the producer's job to convince the studio that the investment is worth it. When Warren Beatty produced *Bonnie and Clyde* for Warners, he was appalled to discover that the studio had no faith in his off-beat gangster movie. Warners opened the movie in two theatres in New York in the middle of the summer, then a notoriously slack time of year in which to release a movie. But despite a conspicuous lack of enthusiasm on the part of the studio, the movie increased its modest box-office take during the second weekend and kept building. Beatty earned his spurs as a producer when he succeeded in persuading Warners to relaunch *Bonnie and Clyde* with a new campaign. The movie became an enormous hit.

If, as sometimes happens, there is a change of management at the studio while the movie is being made, the producer is in trouble. Loretha Jones, who started out in the movie business when she became director Spike Lee's lawyer, suffered as a result of the change of management at Columbia. She was associate

Smash and grab: when Warners gave Bonnie and Clyde *a half-hearted release Warren Beatty, who produced and starred in the movie, forced the studio to relaunch the film with a new campaign.*

Columbia Pictures dumped Spike Lee's School Daze *when the studio's management changed.*

producer on Spike Lee's *School Daze*, a movie which she says David Puttnam planned to open right across the country at 1 200 theatres. Instead, the new regime gave it a small art-house opening and the movie disappeared. In order to avoid the same fate befalling her next movie, *The Five Heartbeats*, Jones and director Robert Townsend went into their pitch meeting with Joe Roth at Twentieth Century Fox armed with a detailed marketing campaign. Their plan was to go back to the old-style Hollywood opening where a publicity roadshow made the launch of the movie a special event in every major city where it premiered. 'We knew that's what was necessary in order to make sure that we didn't shoot a film and then have it on the shelf somewhere and die,' she says. Fox bought the strategy.

Don Simpson and Jerry Bruckheimer take as close an interest in the sales and marketing strategy for releasing their films as they do in the making of them. The two partners, described by Bruckheimer as 'different parts of the same brain', divide the chores between them. Bruckheimer is a details man; Simpson is the long-range strategist. When they decided that Paramount, the studio for whom they produced the hit movies, *Flashdance* and *Top*

When the time came to pitch The Five Heartbeats *to Twentieth Century Fox, director Robert Townsend (centre) came armed with a detailed marketing campaign as well as a script.*

Gun, had missed out on exploiting the merchandizing potential for leg-warmers, ripped T-shirts and flyer jackets, they forced the studio to create a new merchandizing unit.

Simpson and Bruckheimer set out to make mainstream commercial movies which are designed to appeal to the largest possible audience. 'Who wants to schlep out, get babysitters, pay $10 to park, $100 for dinner, $20 for tickets and then leave the theatre feeling like killing yourself?' says Simpson. 'Jerry and I are our own consumers. We have been very fortunate in that we are the audience. That may change some day, but for now, our point of view is the audience point of view.' Together they produced *Beverly Hills Cop, Top Gun* and *Beverly Hills Cop II*, which were the highest grossing movies of 1984, 1986 and 1987. Their movies have generated more than $2 billion in sales of theatre tickets, video cassettes and record albums around the world. Simpson and Bruckheimer pay a great deal of attention to the soundtracks of their movies – to good effect. Three of their soundtrack albums – for *Flashdance, Beverly Hills Cop*, and *Top Gun* – have made the Number One spot. Music to Simpson is 'like a coat of wax on a beautiful car'. And although their movies have been ignored by the Academy, two of their title songs – *What a Feeling* and *Take My Breath Away* – have won Oscars.

'It's always a real nervous feeling when you've worked on something for a minimum of two years and it all depends on two weekends,' says Bruckheimer. 'You pretty much know what you have after the second.weekend. Nobody really has a crystal ball; nobody knows how good the picture really is until the public says, "Hey, that was great!"' Simpson and Bruckheimer always planned to release *Days of Thunder*, a racing movie starring Tom Cruise, in the summer of 1990. Problems piled up during production, the movie shot over-budget and the period set aside for post-production had to be squeezed to accommodate Paramount's opening date. Once *Days of Thunder* was ready to roll, it had to stand up against a host of blockbusters from rival studios – *Total Recall, Die Hard II, Dick Tracy* ... almost one a week during the peak-playing period. 'This summer it's a whole different ballgame,' admitted Simpson. 'In all the years that I have been in Hollywood, it's always been axiomatic that while distribution and marketing enhance a movie that is good, it's still the movie itself that makes or breaks it. Well, that's still true to a degree, but this summer the dynamic of the movie business has changed. In the first time in their history, movies have become more marketing driven. If you look at the money that was spent to promote and advertize the movie, you will see a direct correlation in the [box-office] business. Without exception the pictures fall into line relative to their expenditures. That's never happened before.' Simpson and Bruckheimer don't have to worry whether the studio is going to put its weight behind selling the movies they make. They have the muscle to ensure the studio spends the bucks. But for most producers, especially those who make movies that are not high-concept, it's an on-going battle to secure an adequate release. The selling never stops. And, as the costs of movie production and movie marketing increase year by year, making the sale only gets tougher.

CHAPTER SEVEN

PIGGIES IN THE MIDDLE

Our relationship with agents can be summed up in a sentence: We pray they don't kill us in our sleep.

Howard Rodman, screenwriter

Decent agents don't like to kill somebody, because there is continuity in this business.

William Goldman, screenwriter

A screenwriter returns home from work to find the police have cordoned off his street. When he explains that this is where he lives the cops let him through. Moments later it becomes clear why they are there – his house has burned to the ground. 'My God! What happened?' the screenwriter says to a police captain standing nearby. 'I'm sorry,' the captain replies, 'your agent came here this afternoon, raped your wife, murdered your children, and torched your house.' The screenwriter looks stunned. 'My *agent* came to my *house*?!'

This joke appeared in *Esquire* magazine along with the footnote: 'WARNING! May be offensive to agents.' Of course, it's unlikely any agent would take umbrage because (a) agents are notorious for the thickness of their skins – it's a prerequisite for the job – and (b) the joke, while seeming to be at their expense, is in fact a veiled compliment. The simple point the punchline makes is that the client depends far more on the agent than the agent depends on the client. Movie stars may fall out of fashion, screenwriters may dry up, studio chiefs will most assuredly be fired but agents are forever. They are the eternal middlemen, brokering the talent of others in return for 10 per cent of their income. 'We measure our worth by our agents' clout,' says screenwriter, Howard Rodman. 'We live in dread of being dropped by them. We gauge our potency by their aggressiveness, our status by the alacrity with which they return our calls. We live in fear of the resentment our agents must harbour towards us for taking 90 per cent of the money they earn.' In other words, the joke is on the client.

Agents are often perceived as the bogeymen of Hollywood. Like bankers and lawyers, they are absolutely necessary and they are resented, even feared because of it. Their code is said to be that of the mafia. They wield their power behind closed doors. They work in the shadows. They are mute before the outside world. Speaking out is considered unseemly. Secrecy is an integral part of their tradecraft. Professionally, they live and die by who and what they know. They trade in information exchanged over the telephone, murmured in restaurants, whispered at private screenings, at parties, at sporting events. In the late eighties, agents began to acquire similar accoutrements and the same allure as Wall Street brokers – the multi-million dollar deals, the gargantuan fees, the celebrity names, the designer life style. Within the industry, some of them are more famous, more feared, than their clients.

Agents are truly powerful because they are the indispensable intermediaries between two hostile camps: Money and Talent. According to agent, Jeremy Zimmer, 'The studios need the talent and the talent needs the studios and everybody sort of pretends they don't need each other, and that's kind of where the agent comes in.' The needs of each camp are invariably in conflict. Money needs

Talent because Money wants to make a profit. Talent needs Money because Talent wants to make art (and get paid for it). Neither speaks the language of the other. They need an interpreter. 'Businessmen and artists sometimes have a difficult time communicating with each other,' admits agent Martin Bauer. 'They have different sensibilities, different interests. An artist's interest is to make the best film he can make. And a studio executive's interest is to make the most money he can make. Sometimes those interests converge, and sometimes they diverge. The great agent is the person who can keep both sides talking.'

Agents are necessary. Howard Rodman likens having an agent to having a membership card to a select club. 'The ability to say, "Call my agent", means that you're a professional. It gets you in the door, makes you acceptable to studios and producers. In a sense, because agents decide who is acceptable to them as a client, they function as the first level of screening for studios and producers in deciding who's legitimate and who's just weird. Above and beyond that, as a screenwriter I am the last person in the world who knows my worth in the marketplace and the job of my agent is to put his shoulder to the door and establish that worth firmly. Most of the agent's work is known as "defending the quote" which is to say, getting my salary up to a certain point and then making sure that I don't do anything foolish like take a job for less than that because I really want to.'

However, agents need clients as much as clients need to be represented by agents. An agent's status in the community and his potency as a dealmaker is measured according to the quality of his client list. Agents spend much of their time courting potential clients. The client, lonely, insecure or on the rebound from another agent, is only too willing to be seduced. But as often as not, once the deed is done client and agent find themselves locked in a marriage of mutual dependency and distrust. The working life of an agent is charged with tension and it's one of Hollywood's sweetest ironies that much of this tension springs from the agent's relationship with his or her own client. Invariably the relationship is more than merely professional. The client is making an emotional investment in the agent. All the client's hopes and expectations are expressed through the agent and it is the job of the agent not only to get the client work at the right price, but to also realize those hopes and expectations. Clients need their agents with varying degrees of desperation and many clients resent their agents because they are embarrassed by their dependency.

The emotional investment the client makes in his or her agent is often reciprocated by the agent. Agents empathize closely with their clients. Some of them may have become agents in the first place because they lacked the talent to act or write themselves and so they opted to live vicariously through the achievements of others. Take Ed Limato, one of Hollywood's leading actor's agents – his clients include Mel Gibson, Richard Gere, Michelle Pfeiffer, Matthew Modine and Nicholas Cage. Limato originally dreamed of being a movie star but he says he never quite had the guts to do it. 'I think that in the beginning a young agent lives through the success of his clients. You need to be a part of what they want to achieve. That's very important.'

The corollary to the vicarious pleasure an agent takes in a client's success is the pain the agent feels when the client fails. Many agents will say that the toughest part of their job is having to deal with their client's inevitable disappointments. 'The toughest part of my job is getting my clients through failure,' says agent Peter Benedek. 'It's very painful. There's a lot at stake. There's a lot of personal hurt that is involved and it takes an enormous amount of time and energy to help a client become resilient enough to bounce back from failure. Failure is the toughest part of this business and most movies fail.'

Dealing with failure is especially tricky for an agent because one

Peter Benedek says that dealing with failure is the toughest part of an agent's job.

way in which a client bounces back from failure is to fire the agent. It's not difficult to understand why. After all, there's a real attraction in responding to rejection by attributing it to the incompetence of someone else rather than to your own shortcomings. Killing the messenger may not change anything but at least it might make you feel better. Agents know this. That's one reason why they become so emotional when they don't get their own way. They're fighting for their lives. As for the client, at the back of his mind, he knows that the agent knows this, and that knowledge only confirms his darkest suspicions. Clients are naturally insecure – most creative people fear rejection – and this insecurity is nourished by the fact that most agents have more than one client. Every client suspects that these other clients have a greater claim on the agent's attention and energies than he or she does.

The paranoia of their clients ensures that most agents are notoriously press shy. When confronted by a working journalist, they invariably turn coy. They exist to serve their clients, not to attract attention for themselves, they say. But agents are equally non-committal when they are asked to comment on one of their own clients. Even compliments can be hard to extract from their tightly welded lips. The reason for this is that agents fear their own clients more than anything else. By not talking to the Press they are trying to protect themselves from the client. They know that if they talk to the Press about a client, some other client will feel neglected, snubbed, resentful, and the hapless agent may well end up being fired because of it. Dealing with a client's suspicions is an occupational hazard of agenting but often those suspicions fester in silence. Maybe the agent hasn't fought the studio as hard as he might have to get you that part because there's another part, a juicier, more lucrative role, that the studio is offering to another client, and your faithless agent can get better terms for that client if he or she sacrifices your interest. It may sound like paranoia but that doesn't mean it's not happening to you right now.

'It's always been my contention that in a town of liars, you need at least two or three people who tell you the truth,' says screenwriter, Roger Simon. 'One of those might be a wife or a girlfriend and the other might be your agent. I know this is sentimental of me, but I would prefer my agent to tell me the truth.' Some time ago Simon ditched his agent because he believed that his trust was misplaced. 'My agent's agency was representing me and it was also representing a director with whom I was making a deal. While the director was on vacation in Mexico, my agent insisted that if I didn't take a certain fee for the movie, the director would go to a different writer. When the director got back from his vacation, I told him this story and he practically fell off his chair. The agent had totally lied. And probably the reason he lied is to score points with the studio. Because, of course, the agent would prefer to be on good terms with the studio than with most of his clients, certainly any writer client, because no writer generates the kind of income that the agencies get from the studios. I mean, that's where they make their money. So ironically, an agent is not really your agent, he's the studio's agent.'

There is that sense in which an agent's bread and butter depends on the buyer, the studio executive. The agent has to take care of the studio. He or she has to keep the studio's executives groomed and fattened up and that may happen at the expense of the client. But clients do not suffer as a result of this kind of conflict of interest as much as they might fear because the tension between the studio and the agent is even greater than that which exists between the agent and the client.

The relationship between agents and studios has been a tense one ever since agents began to challenge the studios for control of the movie business. They've been squabbling about it ever since 1949. That was the year that an agent, Jules Cesar Stein, forced Warner Brothers boss, Jack Warner, to release his most precious star, Bette Davis, from a contract which still had a full ten years left to run. For Warner – the man who is reputed to have said of his contract artists, 'I pay 'em. They do what I tell 'em,' – it was the end of an era. A year later, Stein scored a second coup when he made Universal give the actor James Stewart a hefty profit share in the movie, *Winchester '73*. Universal had already suffered the indignity of releasing Stewart from his contract and now the studio found itself forced to make a deal with the star that eventually earned him some $600 000.

Jules Stein changed the nature of the entertainment business. The agency he founded in 1924, the Music Corporation of America (MCA), grew to be so powerful that it became known as the 'star-spangled octopus'. Stein began by booking bands around the country before making his move on Hollywood. From the start, he set out to sign up the big names. Bette Davis was his first major client. Errol Flynn, John Garfield and Paul Henreid followed. In 1945, Stein bought the client list of one of Hollywood's leading agents, Leland

Pay dirt: agent Jules Stein negotiated a hefty profit share in the movie, Winchester '73, *for his client James Stewart.*

Hayward. Hayward's clients, who now belonged to MCA, not only included some of the best writers and directors then working in Hollywood – Ben Hecht and Dashiell Hammett, Billy Wilder and William Wyler – but also an extraordinary galaxy of stars: James Stewart, Henry Fonda, Gene Kelly, Boris Karloff, Greta Garbo, Fred Astaire, Katharine Hepburn...

Within a decade, Stein and his protégé, Lew Wasserman, had made MCA the single most powerful organization in show business. As the contract system crumbled, the studios were forced to compete for talent in an open market. Star salaries went through the roof and 10 per cent of those stratospheric earnings went to MCA. But 10 per cent was not enough for Stein. MCA moved into production and, thanks to the good graces of Ronald Reagan, Stein went on to make a killing in television. In 1952, Reagan, then president of the

A galaxy of stars: when the likes of Henry Fonda and Bette Davis signed with Stein, his agency became known as the 'star-spangled octopus'.

Garbo speaks! – But only through her agent, Jules Cesar Stein.

Screen Actors Guild, granted MCA an exclusive waiver, exempting the agency from the rule which barred agents from working as producers. Reagan's waiver allowed MCA to become the biggest supplier of primetime programming to the networks. Then in 1959 MCA bought Universal Studios.

MCA's grip on the industry had become so tight that three years later the Justice Department moved in on the 'star-spangled octopus'. Stein pre-empted their intervention by closing the agency. The serious money, he decided, was to be made in production. He stepped back from day-to-day involvement and left Lew Wasserman to run Universal. The vacuum created by the closure of the agency was swiftly filled by a new generation of agents. Many of them were alumni of MCA and they applied Stein's methods with the zeal of disciples who expected to inherit the earth, or at least that portion of it devoted to the entertainment business. Ever since, studios and

A mogul is born: when Lew Wasserman inherited Jules Stein's empire he became the most powerful man in movies. Today, Mike Ovitz is said to cherish that mantle.

agents have been battling it out for the upper hand.

Today, if agents don't actually run Hollywood, and the Press loves to hint that they do, then they are certainly card-carrying members of the town's ruling oligarchy. The most powerful of them are, if not exactly moguls, then at least second cousins to the old studio chieftains, and the lists of their clients are the closest Hollywood comes today to the contract players of old. 'The studio abrogated control after the moguls were gone,' says producer Bernie Brillstein. 'When Spencer Tracy [who was under contract to Louis B. Mayer at MGM] wanted to make a movie for Columbia, he had to beg Mayer to let him. Today if a studio wants someone it better have a good relationship with CAA.'

    CAA – Creative Artists Agency – is widely recognized as Hollywood's hottest agency. Their client list, some 600 strong, would make Louis B. Mayer puff with pride. It features an incredible collection of 'bankable' names. CAA's stable of stars includes Dustin Hoffman, Sylvester Stallone, Bill Murray, Barbra Streisand, Robert Redford, Paul Newman, Kevin Costner, Robert De Niro, Jane Fonda, Al Pacino, Robin Williams, Sally Field, Dan Aykroyd, Chevy Chase, Glenn Close, Michael Keaton, Sean Connery, Tom Cruise, Gene Hackman, Goldie Hawn, Bette Midler and Cher. The directors on CAA's roster are some of the biggest names in Hollywood: Sydney Pollack (*Tootsie, Out of Africa, Havana*), Steven Spielberg (*Jaws, Close Encounters of the Third Kind, ET*), Oliver Stone (*Platoon, Wall Street, Born on the Fourth of July*), Robert Zemeckis (*Who Framed Roger Rabbit? Back to the Future I, II and III*), Ron Howard (*Splash, Cocoon, Parenthood*), Martin Scorsese (*Taxi Driver, Raging Bull, Good Fellas*), David Lynch (*Blue Velvet, The Elephant Man*) and Barry Levinson (*Diner, Good Morning Vietnam, Rain Man*).

But, as impressive as its list of clients may be, Creative Artists does not possess anything like the monopoly of talent that MCA enjoyed at its peak. The power that was once absolute to MCA is now fragmented among a host of competitors. Today Hollywood's agencies are divided into two distinct tiers. At one level you have the Big Three: William Morris, International Creative Management (ICM), and the relatively young Creative Artists. On the second tier are the so-called 'boutique' agencies who trade on a select handful of important clients. Among the boutique agencies, Bauer-Benedek (whose clients include actor Michael J. Fox, director Brian De Palma and writer-director Lawrence Kasdan) is probably the most prominent, but the newly minted Inter-Talent, founded by ICM renegade Bill Bloch, is catching up fast. 'There have been some radical changes in the power structure of the agency business,' explains attorney Peter Dekom. 'The old line large agencies that have been around for a long time have found themselves challenged quite severely by not only new large agencies that have loomed up [namely CAA], but a number of small boutiques that have taken some pretty terrific clients into representation. That's a relatively new phenomenon. And I suspect that the level of competition will only increase in the future.'

'I would say that the competition between agencies in Hollywood today is as rough as I've ever seen it,' says Martin Bauer. The competition is so tough because the stakes in Hollywood have risen so substantially over the last few years. The economics have changed. Salaries have risen to the $1 million to $2 million category for many directors. Some get $3 million to $4 million. The average quasi-bankable actor will get $2 million and some of the superstars will get between $5 million and $10 million. The agency business has become very lucrative and a lot of people are trying to get into that business.

According to *Variety*, the pitch of competition has made Hollywood as peaceful as downtown Beirut. Signing clients is at the heart of the agency business and the competition between agents to sign the hot names is frenzied and sometimes unscrupulous. 'The big agencies are like animals, raping and pillaging one another day in and day out,' says Jeremy Zimmer. 'We're all out there doing business. It's very competitive. And at the end of the day the question is always who's doing what to whom, how much are they doing it for, and when are they going to do it to me.' Zimmer, a young and successful literary agent at ICM, addressed these candid remarks to an audience of independent filmmakers. 'It's a very aggressive culture and Jeremy came out and said it,' says Michael Cieply who reports regularly on the Borgia-like working habits of Hollywood's leading agents for the *Los Angeles Times*. 'He spoke what was the truth. It was a very unseemly truth. There were objections.' Zimmer's remarks subsequently appeared in *Daily Variety*, prompting a public apology from ICM boss, Jeff Berg, followed by Zimmer's resignation from the agency shortly thereafter. He is now a partner at Bauer-Benedek.

The older generation of agents are astounded by the change. 'I don't really like the way the business has gone,' says the veteran actors' agent, Ed Limato. 'Getting new clients nowadays has become a very predatory thing.' When a potentially hot client arrives in town he or she is besieged by ten or fifteen agents. During that period, when agents are trying to sign a client, the activity is frenetic. Michael Caton-Jones, a young British director, arrived in Hollywood shortly after his first movie, *Scandal*, was received with acclaim. At the time, he didn't have an agent and when he checked into his hotel, he was astounded by the enormous pile of gifts that had been sent by solicitous agents who were competing to represent him. Says one agent at the ultra-competitive CAA, 'You need to keep signing the hot new faces, the flavour of the month, so the old ones will continue to believe they're in the right place. CAA just got Kevin Costner from [William] Morris, so Sydney Pollack has to think, "Yes, this is the best agency."'

Generally speaking, agencies compete with other agencies within their own peer group. 'Competition between agents is ferocious but there are rules of engagement even though every rule seems to be made to be broken,' says Cieply. 'For a very long time CAA had an unwritten rule that they would never raid a smaller agency and particularly would never take a bread and butter client away from a small agency. The other rule at Creative Artists was that they would raid William Morris consistently. There was an absolute hatred that seemed to set in between the two agencies.'

The bloody battle between the venerable William Morris Agency – founded more than a hundred years ago – and the upstart CAA has raged for some fifteen years. Like many executives who now occupy positions of power in Hollywood, CAA president, Michael Ovitz, began his career in the Morris mailroom. He swiftly rose up through

the agency. But Morris's ruling Politburo of elder statesmen effectively capped the rise of younger talents and Ovitz grew frustrated.
He was not alone. When word leaked out that Ovitz and four other
Morris men were planning to set up on their own, the five agents
were fired. Their Creative Artists Agency opened for business swiftly
thereafter and, despite the attempts of William Morris to crush the
fledgling agency, CAA survived and prospered and fought back.

Ovitz had cut his teeth at William Morris putting together television shows for the networks and television was the foundation
upon which CAA established itself in the early years. As CAA was
struggling to find its feet, Ovitz cultivated close relations with the
powerful New York literary agent, Morton Janklow, whose clients
include novelists Judith Krantz, Jackie Collins and Danielle Steel,
all of whom produce the kind of best-selling door-stoppers that are
ideal source material for the hundred hours or so of mini-series
fodder Ovitz is said to have 'packaged' for the networks as a result
of his association with Janklow. Packaging refers to the practice of
putting together a television series by forging an alliance between a
literary property or a writer and a number of clients – say a director
and one or two actors – and then selling it to the networks. Instead
of earning just 10 per cent of a client's salary, the agency which
packages the show traditionally takes 10 per cent of the network
licensing fee plus a further 5 per cent of revenues from subsequent
sales to the syndication market and abroad. But whereas William
Morris charged the usual 10 per cent fee for packaging television
shows, CAA slashed its fee to 6 per cent.

Over the last decade, the older agency has been bleeding badly.
The glory days when William Morris represented such Hollywood
greats as Charlie Chaplin, Al Jolson, Mae West, Marilyn Monroe,
Elvis Presley and Frank Sinatra are long past. Morris is still strong
in the television market, thanks to the money it earns by managing
such lucrative series as *The Cosby Show*. But the movie division has

lost some of its best people. Ovitz and Co. were not the only agents to jump ship. In their wake, Martin Bauer left to set up Bauer-Benedek – taking directors Brian De Palma and John Avildsen and actor Alan Alda with him – and Ed Limato recently defected to ICM together with a valuable clutch of star clients including Mel Gibson and Richard Gere. The death of Stanley Kamen, the venerable Morris man who represented Goldie Hawn, Barbra Streisand, Warren Beatty, Diane Keaton and Chevy Chase among others, was a severe blow to the agency. In the five years since then, Morris has failed to find its momentum. 'How do you commit the perfect murder?' runs the Hollywood joke. 'Kill your wife and go to work for William Morris. They'll never find you.'

By contrast, Creative Artists has thrived, so much so that when *Premiere* magazine ranked the top one hundred names in Hollywood, no one was very surprised when they gave the Number One spot to CAA's president, Michael Ovitz. Agents generally stay in the wings but no one is so deliberately invisible as the CAA boss. When Dustin Hoffman accepted his Best Actor Oscar for *Rain Man*, he made sure to thank his agent, Michael Ovitz, for his tireless efforts in bringing the movie to fruition. For the CAA president it was a rare and probably unwelcome moment in the spotlight. Ovitz is notoriously shy of publicity and, as there are few subjects closer to a journalist's heart than a powerful recluse, this has assured him front-page profiles in the *New York Times Magazine* and the calendar section of the *Los Angeles Times* as well as a meaty spread in *Time*. It's one of the ironies of CAA, and one must assume it's no accident that, while the agency professes to shun publicity of any kind, CAA receives more media exposure than all its competitors put together. 'The man with the golden thumb', as *Time* dubbed him, is generally reckoned to be the closest equivalent in Hollywood today to the old moguls, a latter-day cocktail of one-part Jules Stein to two-parts Lew Wasserman with maybe a dash of Sun Tzu.

One happy family: CAA clients (from left to right) producer Mark Johnson, stars Tom Cruise and Dustin Hoffman, and director Barry Levinson bask in the Academy Award-winning glory of Rain Man. *During his acceptance speech, Hoffman credited his agent, Mike Ovitz, with making the movie happen.*

Sun Tzu is the author of the classic Chinese manual of military tactics, *The Art of War*, which is said to be something of a management bible at CAA. Ovitz, a student of Oriental philosophy and an aikido enthusiast, favours a *mélange* of Eastern and Western management techniques. 'Some companies believe that internal competition helps the bottom line, but I'm not of that school,' he says. 'We try to take the paternal approach of the Japanese, who take care of their own, and temper that with Western creativity and ingenuity.' While agents at William Morris and ICM, CAA's two great rivals, often operate as lone wolves who just happen to share the same roof, Ovitz and his colleagues have made team spirit a religion. CAA does not recruit its agents, it converts them. When they go to meetings at CAA, some clients feel as if they are dealing with the disciples of some arcane cult. 'The opening interview can be a little claustrophobic,' says one. 'You're in a room with about five agents, and you get a complete rap from every one of them for about two hours. At the end of mine, the woman agent broke down and cried because CAA was such a great place to work.'

You only have to enter CAA's new corporate headquarters, designed by the Chinese architect I. M. Pei, to sense that the agency is quite unlike any of its rivals. The atrium – which is dominated by a 28-foot-high painting by the pop artist, Roy Lichtenstein – is designed to impress, even intimidate. People seem insignificant in this cathedral of marble and glass. The CAA building is a monument

The Sun (Tzu) also rises: director Sydney Pollack with his agent, Mike Ovitz, the boss of Creative Artists Agency.

to a modern corporation. And like the Orientals, Ovitz places a high premium on corporate loyalty. 'If you leave Creative Artists,' says a CAA agent, 'we sit shiva for seven days ... and then you die.'

So far, the most dramatic act of client 'disloyalty' has been the defection of Joe Eszterhas. Eszterhas, a journalist-turned-screen-writer, whose portfolio includes the scripts for such successful movies as *Flashdance*, *Jagged Edge*, *Music Box* and *Betrayed*, was represented by Michael Ovitz. But towards the end of 1989, Eszterhas decided to switch agents. He wanted to move back to his old friend, Guy McElwaine, who had represented him earlier in his career. McElwaine, a publicist-turned-agent-turned-studio executive-turned-agent, had recently moved back to his old agency, ICM, as vice-chairman. Eszterhas met Ovitz to tell him that he was leaving CAA for ICM. What happened next is the subject of some dispute. According to a letter sent by a shaken Eszterhas to Ovitz some days after their meeting, the CAA president threatened that if Eszterhas quit, his 'foot soldiers' would 'blow [his] brains out'. Eszterhas also quoted Ovitz as saying: 'This town is like a chess game. ICM isn't going after a pawn or a knight, they're going after a king. If the king goes, the knights and pawns will follow.'

Within days Hollywood's electronic grapevine was humming. Fax machines in offices all over town chattered out copies of Eszterhas's letter which had been mysteriously leaked. Extracts from the letter were published in the *Los Angeles Times* and the *Herald Examiner*. Ovitz wrote back to Eszterhas, refuting his allegations. In December, two magazines – *Premiere* and *Spy* – published the Eszterhas-Ovitz correspondence in full. For a moment, the incident blossomed from a delicious local scandal into national news. And then it fizzled out.

In retrospect, it's important to see the Eszterhas fracas in context. Colourful language and macho threats are par for the course in Hollywood dealmaking. Agents are notoriously emotional. No one seriously believes that Joe Eszterhas's life was ever in any real danger.

What is more significant is that publication of the letter, as the *Los Angeles Times* put it, seemed 'to have tapped into an underlying resentment towards CAA'. Following publication, the paper received half a dozen calls alleging similar treatment at the hands of the agency. But significantly, even in the wake of the Eszterhas letter, the complaints were cloaked in anonymity.

If there is any truth to the events as Eszterhas described them, then there are two possible reasons why Ovitz fought so fiercely to keep his client. The first is the feverish competition that characterizes the agency business today. Losing a high-profile client such as Eszterhas is the kind of publicity any agency could do without. The second reason is that Eszterhas was not just an important client, he was a screenwriter who was especially valuable to the agency. Eszterhas was one of a handful of writers who had consistently produced commercial screenplays, in other words screenplays that attracted star names. The last three Eszterhas scripts generated meaty star roles for Glenn Close and Jeff Bridges (*Jagged Edge*), Debra Winger (*Betrayed*) and Jessica Lange (*Music Box*), all of whom were clients of CAA. Losing Eszterhas was a blow to an agency which had built and consolidated its power by representing writers. Just how big a blow it was became apparent some months later when Eszterhas's new screenplay, *Basic Instinct*, was sold for $3 million.

'Look at the letterhead of the CAA stationery,' says Tony Ludwig, a former CAA agent. 'It says, "literary and talent agency". The key is the fact that material comes first. CAA represents an incredible number of screenwriters. They're the foundation that the agency's built on. At CAA, you could get the scripts you wanted.' Scripts are important because they are the first step towards packaging movies. By matching a good screenplay with one or two bankable stars and a hot director, all of whom are CAA clients, the agency can present a studio with a fully formed project which it often finds difficult to refuse.

Packaging is not exclusive to CAA – William Morris has made a fortune by packaging shows for television – but CAA is credited with applying the techniques of television packaging to the movies and it practises that technique more aggressively and with more success than anyone else. An example of CAA's facility at packaging projects is provided by the movie, *Legal Eagles*. The screenplay was originally written by CAA clients, Jim Cash and Jack Epps Jr, for producer-director Ivan Reitman, also a CAA client. CAA clients Dustin Hoffman and Bill Murray were to star in the movie. Hoffman was unavailable and another CAA client, Robert Redford, stepped in. Then Murray dropped out and Debra Winger, a CAA client, was

The package: the writers, stars (Robert Redford and Debra Winger) and director of Legal Eagles *all have one thing in common – their agency.*

cast opposite Redford. The movie, which flopped, ended up costing the studio, in this case Universal, a hefty $35 million. But CAA made a bundle in commissions.

The issue of packaging is somewhat controversial and CAA has been criticized for institutionalizing a practice by which talent is not represented as an individual element but as joint associations, bonded together to command the highest price. Packaging, say the critics, artificially inflates the cost of moviemaking. But the agents alone are not to blame. After all an agent's job is to secure the highest possible price for a client's services. If the price is too high, then it's up to the buyer, the studio, to turn the deal down. 'The studios always have the power,' says agent Louis Pitt. 'They have the ability to say, "Yes." They have the ability to say, "No." They can spend whatever it is they want to spend. We have the ability to accept it or reject it. So the power is really with them.' Agents can use their wits to play the market but ultimately the price of talent is a product of supply and demand. Martin Bauer does not believe that agents are to blame for the increased costs of talent. 'I think that the studios are involved in intensive bidding for talent and I think that, at any one time, each studio will raise the ante by paying a particular person way beyond what the other actors of his stature get and then the agents follow suit. It's usually a company that is in trouble, or perhaps has new management. I think the studios are the primary players who are responsible for costs escalating.'

It is also said that packaging forces filmmakers into associations which are more to the agency's convenience than to the studio's or the producer's. According to producer Richard Zanuck, 'Agents that have top clients are putting their top director with one of their top stars. Maybe you don't want their top director – maybe you have somebody else in mind – but their top star wants their top director, and so if you want the star, you have to take the package.' But the major reason why packaging generates such controversy is because it is said to be the prime technique by which the big agencies have got the upper hand in their decades-old battle with the studios. The argument runs as follows: by manipulating their client lists the big agencies have relegated the studios to little more than finance and facilities houses whose only function is to bankroll and distribute movies which have been initiated from within the agency. CAA, with its sparkling list of clients, is said to be the prime culprit. But packaging, which was never exclusive to CAA in the first place, is practised by other agencies and this has given rise to the notion that the agents have hijacked Hollywood from the studios. Today, so it is said, the 10 per centers run the town.

There is some validity to this argument but not much. Attractive as it may be to conspiracy theorists, it's an over-simplification of what is really a very subtle and complex balance of power between individual studios and individual agencies which is shifting almost day by day. This balance of power depends on a number of factors that are outside the agents' control. Firstly, although agents are powerful, that power is founded on their client list and those clients are not under contract to the agent in the same way as writers, actors and directors were once under contract to the old studio moguls. As much as CAA's client list may evoke the memory of the contract players who were wedded to Darryl Zanuck and his ilk, CAA's president, Michael Ovitz, cannot simply run his finger down that list, as Zanuck might have done, and pick and choose who will work with whom. The more CAA clients work together, the more money the agency makes but CAA has to persuade its clients to work together first.

'I don't think there's much truth in the rumour that we are all beholden to the agents,' says Universal's Tom Pollock. 'I think that the power in Hollywood belongs to the talent.' Agents represent talent, so to the extent that they can control that talent, which is usually not very often, there's power there. But the real power comes from material, meaning screenplays, because all talent is attracted to screenplays. When a studio develops a good screenplay in-house and submits it to a director or an actor, then the studio will usually get them. 'We try to develop films in-house where we can,' says Pollock, 'and what that does is enable us to decide who we want to put in the film as opposed to having third parties like agents bring us large packages where we have less control over who it is. The more we are able to do, the more control we have.'

Agents often enjoy their power by default. For an agent to be strong, the studio must be weak. 'The more successful the studio is, the less vulnerable it is to domination by one or more of the agencies,' says attorney Peter Dekom. 'Weaker studios tend to go to the agencies and say, "What have you got? Please give me something". The minute you say those statements, agents will descend upon that poor hapless studio like sharks in a feeding frenzy.' Frequent changes in management make a studio weak. A new regime at the studio will be under terrific pressure to release movies quickly. Because the new studio boss has not had the time to develop projects, he or she will be tempted to ask the agencies to provide screenplays that come attached with a director and a star or two, ready-made movies, if you will, that only require the addition of large amounts of money to be ready for consumption.

Tom Pollock, whose own studio, Universal, has enjoyed exceptionally stable management, is well aware that in the last ten or fifteen years studios have changed their management with great regularity whereas agencies have enjoyed more continuity. 'It takes years to bring up a new slate of screenplays. Where there is a lack of continuity at a specific studio, you don't have the time to develop the screenplays. You don't have the time to put it all together and make it work because by the time you do, somebody else has come in and thrown out all your screenplays and started to develop their own.' Columbia Pictures is a case in point. When David Puttnam suddenly resigned as chairman, it was generally believed that one reason for his premature departure was his inability to work with the agencies, especially CAA. Puttnam criticized CAA for artificially inflating the costs of moviemaking by exacting such high fees for their clients' services. Partly as a result of this stance, Puttnam was unable to capitalize on the success of one of the studio's few hit movies, *Ghostbusters*. The director, Ivan Reitman, as well as the stars of the movie – Bill Murray, Dan Aykroyd and Harold Ramis – were all CAA clients. Shortly after her arrival as Puttnam's successor, Dawn Steel proudly announced that Columbia was putting *Ghostbusters II* into production. But although it was a coup to put together the very same guaranteed money-making formula which had eluded Puttnam, Steel was criticized for submitting to CAA's terms and making a deal which meant a hefty share of the movie's profits went to CAA clients leaving only a relatively modest sum for Columbia's depleted coffers.

Strong studios with stable management develop their own material in-house and only then do they go to the agencies to staff their movies with the talent of their choice. 'The strength of a company is what it does with its own resources rather than what it buys packaged from somebody else,' says Twentieth Century Fox chairman, Barry Diller. 'A film script that is good will attract the talent you need to be in it despite every single agent in America being against you.' Ned Tanen, who began his career as an agent with MCA before serving as president of two major studios, Universal and Paramount, has no doubt where the power is. 'The companies are running Hollywood because the companies are where the money is, and money runs the business.'

Agents may not run Hollywood but many of the most powerful people in town are or were agents. Lew Wasserman was the first of a new generation of studio executives who cut their teeth in the agency business. Ted Ashley, an agent with William Morris, went on to run Warner Brothers. David Begelman who, with Freddie Fields, founded Creative Management Associates (representing such high-calibre talent as Paul Newman, Steve McQueen and Barbra Streisand) went on to head production at Columbia and then MGM. Fields eventually retired as an agent to become president of MGM/UA. Ned Tanen, who ran production at Universal and then Paramount, was previously an agent with MCA. Mike Medavoy, now chairman of Tri-Star (Columbia's sister company), began his career as an agent at William Morris. Barry Diller, chairman of Fox, started out, like so many Hollywood powerbrokers, in the Morris mailroom. For many agents and ex-agents, the mailroom is where it all began.

Today, the process by which laymen are inducted into the 'masonic lodges' of the Hollywood agencies is still the same as it ever was. A trainee agent serves a two- to three-year apprenticeship which begins with a spell in the agency mailroom. 'The mailroom experience, which seems to be the best way to start out as an agent, is an osmotic process,' says agent Jeremy Zimmer. 'It's sort of like what you learn in the crib. You don't really learn anything that you can say you learned, but you learn what it feels like to be alive. You learn what's safe and what's not safe; what smells right and what doesn't smell right. That's what you learn in the mailroom.' Louis Pitt, a top agent at International Creative Management who represents, among others, Dudley Moore and Arnold Schwarzenegger, explains, 'You learn priorities. The best thing is to be a sponge and absorb all the information you can about who's who, who's where, who's important, who's not important.' Of his time in the William Morris mailroom Barry Diller says, 'My curiosity was somewhat insatiable and I read everything that wasn't nailed shut. I got a great early learning experience about how things work. It was like going to school. It was invaluable.'

The mailroom is about as menial as work gets in Hollywood and fledgling agents do everything they can to claw their way out. The process of advancement is pure Darwinism – survival of the fittest. You 'learn the town' by delivering messages and parcels to clients and studios; you learn the agency by bringing the agents their mail and you fight like hell to make your mark. 'You learn every player in the agency, what they do, when they come in the office, who their clients are, and how they operate,' says Barry Mendel, a young agent at ICM. 'You also begin to see who you want to emulate. You begin to pick role models.' Getting out of the mailroom means marking out the agent you want to work for and charming him or her into hiring you. Jeremy Zimmer is in no doubt about the way he makes his choice. 'When I look for an assistant I look for someone who reminds me of me.'

Two years or so of listening in on your boss's phone calls, scribbling notes at meetings, memorizing every face and fact seen and heard at breakfast, lunch and dinner and maybe you might make it as an agent. 'You learn what an agent sounds like and talks like and dresses like, and how he handles himself,' says Zimmer. 'You see what it' looks like in an agent's office – who's succeeding, who's failing – and you start to understand the rhythms. You need tenacity. You need insight. You need instinct. Before you can acquire the skills of an agent, you have to have the heart and soul of an agent. It's like being a fisherman. You need to be able to look at the water and see if there are any fish underneath it. That's what good agents can do.'

One of the activities a trainee agent observes most keenly is the process of making deals. The popular image of an agent's working day is dominated by the idea that agents spend their time locked in the verbal equivalent of arm wrestling to secure the best deal possible. It's all sweat and muscle. But despite the macho mythology, deal-making is rarely so clear-cut. According to Zimmer, it's different every time. 'You've got your basic "mercy" deal – which is when you throw yourself on the mercy of the other person – to your "you-have-all-the-cards" deal, in which case you just pound the living shit out of the other guy. But remember that you're going to be doing this for a long time. Every time you go out and beat the crap out of somebody remember that today you own the bat but tomorrow the other guy owns the bat and he's going to beat the crap out of you.' 'Use a velvet glove,' says Ed Limato. 'It's very important in Hollywood to be liked, not just to be feared. There are a lot of people who are feared, but most of them don't have durability.' Agents have to keep in mind that there should always be a next step. The key is to keep both sides talking and use one deal to beget the next.

Once the trainee agent has absorbed his mentor's teaching long enough to be confident of emulating the master, then he's ready to begin the subtle dance of mutual dependency that exists at the heart of an agent's life. He starts to fish for information, for clients, for deals. The telephone is the primary tool of working agents. It's the rod and line with which they make their catches. 'I would say ninety-five per cent of my day is spent on the telephone,' says Martin Bauer. 'That phone really is an extension of me,' says Louis Pitt, who makes and takes about 200 calls a day. 'It's odourless. It's colourless. And I've got to project whatever it is I want them to feel over that phone. It's really a nightmare to deal with but it's a necessary evil.'

If the phone is the agent-angler's rod and line, then their favoured ponds, the shallows where the fattest fish can be caught, are the select bunch of 'power' restaurants where information is traded, relationships are formed and deals are struck over breakfast (at the Beverly Hills Hotel's Polo Lounge), lunch (at Le Dome or the Palm) and dinner (at Morton's or Spago's). 'Lunch is part of my working day,' says Peter Benedek. 'It's an opportunity to get to know someone better. I mean, when you can spend two hours with someone, you

Giving good phone: according to Martin Bauer, the great agent is the person who can keep both sides talking.

can accomplish much more than in fifteen minutes on the telephone.' Lunch is a time to exchange information. The key commerce that agents traffic in is information. The reason clients and buyers come to them is for their information about the marketplace. Agents spend their time trafficking in information and lunch is a place where they either acquire or disseminate it.

To observe lunch at Le Dome – Hollywood's premier midday 'eaterie', as *Variety* calls it – is to see the entertainment business in microcosm. It's all gossip and deals. The two are closely related because the buying trends in Hollywood change very quickly and these trends are sometimes based not on merit but on what, in the business, is called heat. As Zimmer explains: 'What makes somebody hot? Somebody else thinking someone's hot, makes somebody hot. It's that simple. You create a relationship between a client and a buyer and you use the fact that that one buyer desires that client to make another buyer desire the same client. And then all of a sudden somebody's vying for them and they're hot.' Deserved or not, a restaurant crowded with industry insiders is the very best way to turn up the heat. 'Talk in Hollywood can make an actor hot,' says Ed Limato. 'Someone with a mouth and a telephone can start a rumour that an actor's hot before anyone's even seen his work. Sometimes it's deserved. Many times it's not.'

Naturally, there are rules to having lunch. The agent goes to the place where the person who has the most prominence wants to have lunch. If it's a studio head, the agent tends to have lunch on the lot. If it's a young production executive and it's a powerful agent, then the executive will tend to come to where the agent is. It's a pecking order. The studios will often pay the bill when they are taking an agent to lunch, because it's a big corporation versus a small business. When an agent is taking his client out to lunch or dinner, the agent picks up the tab, no matter what. According to Martin Bauer, 'If the client tries to pick it up, the agent is required to throw his body on the table to prevent it.'

'The agent seduces you,' says screenwriter Roger Simon. 'Now any intelligent human being knows that when a guy takes you out to lunch and tells you that you're the greatest thing since sliced bread, they're having you on. Of course, the same human being, namely me, is a sucker for it. I was a sucker for it on several occasions. And you know, the better the quality of the lunch and the frequency of the lunches and dinners involved in this mating process, the more seduced you become. And that's how you end up with this great person for your agent, who then typically forgets you the next day.'

Signing clients is, of course, at the very heart of the agency business. The more talented people an agent signs, the more control he has of the business. Ex-agent Freddie Fields breaks agents down into three categories: 'There's the signer; there's what we call the holder, the person that can hold the client once he's been signed;

and then there's the seller. They could be three different people or they could be just one. But the primary person is the person who can sign talent. That is what elevates the power of an agency because like everything else, people want to go where the strength is. If an agency has many powerful actors and directors and writers, then most talented actors, directors and writers will want to go with that agency.' Agents are only as powerful as their clients. But that power can be cumulative and a crafty agent will use the status of one client to the advantage of another. If an agent has three or four top stars who are in constant demand, then the agent is in a powerful position. Even if a buyer – a producer, say – is after one of the agent's lesser clients, one who maybe isn't a star, the agent can still extract a good deal because he knows that producer may well need one of his star clients for his next movie, and the producer knows it too.

Once the client has been signed, the agent has to defend the catch from other hungry predators. It's often just as difficult to hold clients once you have won them as it is to win them in the first place. As Martin Bauer says, 'If the client is doing well, you have a greater chance of keeping him. If his movies succeed, if he's in demand, he tends to be happier with his agent. If his career is going in a southerly direction, he tends to be dissatisfied with his representation. You can often tell whether a client is dissatisfied with another agent by a network of information that flows in this town from the lawyers, from the producers, from the studio executives. Some agents call other agents' clients and try to create dissatisfaction.' The practice of poaching clients by spreading malicious gossip, exacerbating the latent distrust between a rival agent and his client, and thus poisoning their relationship, is increasingly common. 'I don't think it creates the best environment to represent someone in,' says Jeremy Zimmer, 'because if you're representing someone defensively you're looking to the short term and not really being honest about the long-range effects of any project.'

For an agent to retain his client, he has to make sure that his client receives as much money, preferably more, than comparable names in his peer group. If Paramount pays Tom Cruise $10 million to star in one of their movies, then Mel Gibson's agent will be looking to get the same for his client. Agents are always keen to keep their clients happy by securing them an original perk that will set a new precedent. The ultimate financial reward that is prized beyond all else, and which every agent sweats blood to secure, are 'gross points' – a percentage of the movie's box-office revenue. 'The best deal that you can make for any actor is what we call a first dollar gross deal,' says Ed Limato. 'That is when an actor gets a percentage, usually starting at ten per cent, of every dollar that goes into the studio's coffers. That simply means that there is no way the studio can lie to you (about the movie's receipts) or tack on this expense or that expense. When you make that kind of deal for an artist, you know that he's home.'

Gross points are so sought after because the alternative, net points, are virtually worthless. The difference between the two is that gross points equals a share of the revenue the movie returns to the studio, while net points equals a share of any profit the studio makes from the movie after overhead costs and expenses have been deducted. Net profits are a mirage. Overhead costs and expenses are open to interpretation – and it's the studio's accountants who are doing the interpreting. Studios are notoriously tetchy about their accounting practices. The true figures are hard to come by. It was ever thus. Back in the forties, the anthropologist, Hortense Powdermaker, observed, 'In all field work there is usually one piece of esoteric data which is hidden by the natives. Among the Melanesians in the South-west Pacific it is black magic. Among the Hollywood executives it is net profits.' In 1989 the Pulitzer prize-winning humorist, Art Buchwald, tried to gain access to this esoteric data when he and his producer, Alain Bernheim, sued Paramount Pictures for the 19 per cent of the net profits they were due from the movie, *Coming to America*. Paramount claimed that *Coming to America*, a vehicle for the studio's biggest star, Eddie Murphy, was not yet in net profit despite the fact that it had already grossed some $350 million. Buchwald's attorney claimed that Paramount had already made a profit of over $40 million from the movie, which had been masked by the studio's accounting practices.

Agents try to combat the studio's creative accounting practices by either securing a gross dollar deal or forcing the studio to commit to a fat fee. In some cases a canny agent can enjoy the best of both worlds. For his client Arnold Schwarzenegger, ICM agent Louis Pitt secured a meaty $10-million fee for starring in the movie *Total Recall* plus 15 per cent of the gross. An agent's ability to make this kind of 'killer deal' depends on the strength of his clients, his ability to play the market and a degree of luck. The installation of new management at a studio or the arrival on the scene of a new production company, flush with cash and eager to make its mark, generally creates a promising climate for agents to secure top dollars for their clients. 'I once sold a book called *Thy Neighbour's Wife* to United Artists for $2.5 million,' says Martin Bauer. 'At the time, that set the record for the largest book purchase in movies. The interesting thing about that sale, is that UA *wanted* to pay that amount of money. A new management had just come in and they wanted to make a statement that they were major players in the movie business. They wanted to pay $2.5 million. I didn't make them do it. They wanted to do it. What I was, was smart enough to realize it.' When new management arrives at a studio, as one development executive puts it, 'they need to show their bosses and their own egos that they can play with the big boys'. The best agents are adept at encouraging studio executives into a 'mine's bigger than yours' style bidding war that can easily degenerate into a feeding frenzy.

During the first few months of 1990 an unprecedented conjunction of events resulted in one of the most frantic bidding wars in recent memory. Towards the end of 1989, Joe Roth was appointed as the new chief at Twentieth Century Fox with a mandate to triple production to between twenty and twenty-five movies a year. At around the same time, Larry Gordon, the producer of such box-office hits as *48 Hours*, *Die Hard* and *Predator*, announced the formation of a new production company, Largo Entertainment, backed by a $100-million fund from the Japanese electronics company, JVC. A month or so later, Peter Guber and Jon Peters, the producers of *Batman*, were paid a king's ransom to run Columbia Pictures. Then early in the new year, Guber appointed Mike Medavoy, previously the long-serving production chief of Orion, as chairman of Columbia's sister company Tri-Star and hired Frank Price to run Columbia's production activities. The field was set for some fierce competition. It was an agent's dream.

In January, 1990, *Private Lives*, a new novel by Warren Adler, sold for $1.2 million to Tri-Star. According to *Variety*, it was 'allegedly the highest price ever paid in Hollywood for an unpublished manuscript'. Then, *Radio Flyer*, a screenplay by David Mickey Evans, went to Columbia for a reported $1 million. At the end of February, *The Ticking Man*, an action comedy about a bomb disposal expert, was bought by Largo Entertainment for $1 million. In the case of *The Ticking Man*, the agent sent a ticking alarm clock to each of the select band of competing buyers. The message was clear. Time was running out. A deal was done within the day. And a week later, *Ultimatum*, a political thriller by Laurence Dworet and Robert Roy Poole, was snapped up by Touchstone for $1 million. Then, in mid-April, Warner Brothers paid a record breaking $1.75 million for *The Last Boy Scout*, a screenplay by Shane Black, who had previously penned the high-grossing thriller, *Lethal Weapon*. Later that year, that record was smashed when Carolco Pictures paid $3 million for *Basic Instinct*, a new screenplay by Joe Eszterhas. David Hoberman, president of Touchstone, told *Variety* that he attributed the steep rise in prices to the agents. 'They are pretty much in the driver's seat,' he said. 'They're playing the marketplace pretty well.'

The mentality of the agent has become the prevalent way of thinking inside Hollywood, perhaps outside as well. Those who can package the elements – bonding the best writer with the right director and an appropriate star – are applauded for their inspiration. Those who can make the equations come out right – a $10-million advance to a star whose name guarantees a $5-million presale to Japan – are admired for their creative acumen. The men and women who know how to make these deals are the élite. The deal is the thing and in Hollywood today the making of deals has come to be seen as an art form in itself.

Making movies and making deals have always marched hand-in-hand but today the numbers matter more than they ever have before. When newspapers publish a movie's opening grosses in addition to the review, and moviegoers choose what to see according to the top ten box-office winners that week, it is clear that the character of Hollywood's mystique is shifting. News of what goes on in the executive suites of Hollywood's power brokers – $3 million for a screenplay, $10 million for a star, $6.59 billion for a whole company – makes gossip as juicy as the intimate details of a star's sex life. The mystique of Hollywood is as strong as it ever was except that now it feeds not on glamour nor on romance, but on power.

SOURCE NOTES

CHAPTER ONE: CITY OF ANGELS

What Makes Sammy Run? by Budd Schulberg, published by Random House, New York, 1941, fiftieth anniversary edition published in 1990; *The Craft of the Screenwriter* by John Brady, published by Simon & Schuster Inc., New York, 1982; *Hollywood: The Dream Factory* by Hortense Powdermaker, published by Ayer Publications, London, 1951; 'Film is a Collaborative Business', in collected essays, *Some Freaks*, by David Mamet, published by Viking Penguin, a division of Penguin Books, USA Inc., 1989; *Picture* by Lillian Ross, published by Proscenium Publishers Inc., New York, October 1984; *Money into Light, The Emerald Forest, A Diary* by John Boorman, published by Faber and Faber, London, 1985.

Tom Huth, 'Welcome to the L.A. Freeway', *California Magazine*, August 1985; Jeannine Stein, 'Be It Ever So Humongous', *Los Angeles Times*, 1 December 1989; Peter Newcomb, 'The Top 40: The World's Highest Paid Entertainers', *Forbes*, 2 October 1989; Celia Brady, 'There's No Business Like Show Business', *Spy*, January 1990; Paul Rosenfield, 'Classic Anjelica', *Los Angeles Times*, Calendar, 4 February 1990; Angela Janklow, 'Laker Mania', *Vanity Fair*, June 1988; 'An Interview with Jerry Buss', *Orange County Register*, 5 December 1989.

CHAPTER TWO: CLAY FEET AND THE BOTTOM LINE

The Last Tycoon by F. Scott Fitzgerald, Penguin, 1986; 1990. New York: Macmillan, 1977; 1983; *The Studio* by John Gregory Dunne, published by Proscenium Publishers Inc., New York, 1985; *The Movie Brats, How the Film Generation Took Over Hollywood* by Michael Pye and Lynda Myles, published by Holt, Reinhardt and Winston, 1979; *The Hollywood Reporter Book of Box Office Hits* by Susan Sackett, published by Billboard Books, New York, 1990; *Made in Japan, Akio Morita and Sony* by Akio Morita with Edwin

M. Reingold and Mitsuko Shimomura, published by NAL Penguin Inc. (Signet), New York, 1986; *Fast Forward: Hollywood, the Japanese and the Video Wars* by James Lardner, published by W. W. Norton & Company Inc., New York, 1987.

Andrea King, 'Dawn with the wind', *The Hollywood Reporter*, 9 January 1990; Elaine Dutka, 'No More Tomorrows for Dawn Steel at Columbia', *Los Angeles Times*, Calendar, 9 January 1990; Tina Brown, 'Hollywood Knives', *Vanity Fair*, April 1988; Stephen J. Sansweet, 'Few Stay Long in High-Pressure Job Of Movie-Studio Production Chief', *Wall Street Journal*, 20 January 1983; Fred Schruers, 'Crossing Over', *Premiere*, April 1990; Claudia Eller, 'Fox Grapes Of Roth Pour Forth', *Variety*, 25 January 1990; Lisa Gubernick, ' "Barry's been distracted" ', *Forbes*, 8 January 1990; Anne Thompson, 'Field of Dream$', *Film Comment*, March/April 1990; Kathleen A. Hughes, 'Going for Broke. Hunt for Blockbusters Has Big Movie Studios In a Spending Frenzy', *Wall Street Journal*, 3 May 1989; Bill Saporito, 'The Inside Story of Time Warner', *Fortune*, 20 November 1989; Connie Bruck, 'Deal of the Year', *The New Yorker*, 8 January 1990; David Lieberman, 'Racing to Keep Up with the Murdochs', *Business Week*, 20 March 1989; Lee Smith, 'Fear and Loathing of Japan', *Fortune*, 26 February 1990; John Schwartz, Joshua Hammer, Michael Reese and Bill Powell, 'Japan Goes Hollywood', *Newsweek*, 9 October 1989; Janice Castro, 'From Walkman to Showman', *Time*, 9 October 1989; Barbara Rudolph, 'Hollywood or Bust', *Time*, 4 September 1989; Will Tusher, 'Japanese go Hollywood with JVC-Gordon venture', *Variety*, 23–29 August 1989; Richard Turner, 'How Larry Gordon Got His $100 Million Movie Deal', *Wall Street Journal*, 23 August 1989; Christine Gorman, 'Dynamic Duos Don't Come Cheap', *Time*, 6 November 1989; Nina J. Easton, 'Behind the Scenes of the Big Deal', *Los Angeles Times*, Calendar, 31 December 1989; Diane K. Shah, 'The Producers', *New York Times Magazine*, 22 October 1989; Lawrence Cohn, 'Exec Shifts Make Columbia The Gem Of Commotion', *Variety*, 22 November 1989; Aljean Harmetz, 'On Feeling Underpaid at $1 Million', *New York Times*, 26 November 1989; John Grenwald, 'Shooting the works: Lights! Camera! Money! Hollywood is on a spree!', *Time*, 21 May 1990.

CHAPTER THREE: HEAVENLY BODIES

Adventures in the Screen Trade by William Goldman, published by Warner Books, New York, 1983; *Memo from David O. Selznick*, selected and edited by Rudy Behlmer, published by Samuel French, Hollywood, 1989; *The*

Genius of the System, by Thomas Schatz, published by Pantheon Books, a division of Random House, New York, 1988.

Joshua Hammer and Andrew Murr, 'The Blockbuster Game', *Newsweek*, 25 June 1990; Howard G. Chua-Eoan, 'Movie Muscle', *Time*, 28 May 1990; Ronald Grover, 'Fat Times for Studios, Fatter Times for Stars', *Business Week*, 24 July 1989; Elaine Dutka, 'Meryl Streep Attacks Hollywood's Gender Gap at SAG Conference', *Los Angeles Times*, 3 August 1990; Terri Minsky, 'The Feminine Mystique', *Premiere*, December 1989; James Ulmer, 'Actresses lose war of sexes at international box office', *Hollywood Reporter*, 26 December 1989; Teresa Carpenter, 'The Self-Made Man', *Premiere*, January 1989; Elizabeth Kaye, 'American Dreamer', *Smart*, May 1990; Jeff Everson, 'Total Recall', *Muscle & Fitness*, July 1990; Alan Richman, 'Arnold Meets the Girly Man', *GQ*, May 1990; Nancy Griffin, 'Mars Needs Arnold', *Premiere*, June 1990; *Entertainment Weekly*, 8 June 1990; Lynn Hirschberg, 'Making It Big', *Vanity Fair*, June 1990; Charles Fleming, 'Star-hungry mags find flacks flexing muscles', *Variety*, 4 July 1990.

CHAPTER FOUR: SCHMUCKS WITH APPLES

Some Freaks by David Mamet, published by Viking Penguin, a division of Penguin Books, USA Inc., 1989; *The Craft of the Screenwriter* by John Brady, published by Simon & Schuster Inc., New York, 1982; *A Child of the Century* by Ben Hecht, published by Simon and Schuster, New York, 1954; *The American Cinema, Directors and Directions, 1929–1968* by Andrew Sarris, The University of Chicago Press, Chicago, 1968; 'Who Makes The Movies?' in a collection of essays, *Pink Triangle and Yellow Star*, by Gore Vidal, published by William Heinemann Ltd, London, 1982.

Michael Cieply, 'Film Studios' Bidding War Creating $1-Million Scripts', *Los Angeles Times*, 19 April 1990; Claudia Eller, 'New Hollywood Chapter Unfolds', *Daily Variety*, 25 June 1990; Nina J. Easton, 'Eszterhas vs. Verhoeven', *Los Angeles Times*, 23 August 1990; Jack Mathews, '$20-Million Lawsuit Filed Over "Look Who's Talking"', *Los Angeles Times*, 24 January 1990; Monica Zurowski, 'Lucas Testifies in Calgary Court That "Jedi" Ewoks Were His Idea', *Los Angeles Times*, 19 January 1990; Nina J. Easton, '"Superman" Lawsuit Trial Date Set for April 16', *Los Angeles Times*, 1 February 1990; Dennis McDougal, 'Buchwald Going to Court Over "Coming to America"', *Los Angeles Times*, 11 December 1989; Elizabeth Guider, 'Writers flex their muscles thanks to Buchwald win', *Variety*, 17 January 1990.

CHAPTER FIVE: HUSTLER-ARTISTS

'Directors and Directing' by David Thomson, an essay in *Anatomy of the Movies*, edited by David Pirie, published by Macmillan Publishing Co., 1981; *Directing the Film: Film Directors on Their Art* by Eric Sherman for The American Film Institute, published by Little, Brown and Co., New York, 1976; 'The Director', by Sydney Pollack, in collected essays, *The Movie Business Book*, edited by Jason E. Squire, published by Columbus Books, London, 1986; *Skywalking, The Life and Films of George Lucas* by Dale Pollock, published by Elm Tree Books, Hamish Hamilton Ltd, 1983; *Filmmakers on Filmmaking, Volume 1* edited by Joseph McBride for The American Film Institute, published by J. P. Tarcher, 1983; 'A First-Time Film Director', in collected essays, *Some Freaks*, by David Mamet, published by Viking Penguin, a division of Penguin Books, USA Inc., 1989; *Money into Light, The Emerald Forest, A Diary* by John Boorman, published by Faber and Faber, London, 1985; *The Genius of the System* by Thomas Schatz, published by Pantheon Books, a division of Random House, New York, 1989; *Coppola* by Peter Cowie, published by André Deutsch Ltd, London, 1989; *Working in Hollywood* by Alexander Brouwer and Thomas Lee Wright, published by Crown Publishers Inc., New York, 1990; *Icons: Intimate Portraits*, by Denise Worrell, published by The Atlantic Monthly Press, New York, 1989.

Audie Bock, 'Zoetrope and Apocalypse Now', *American Film*, September 1979; Michael Cieply, 'Coppola Seeks Bankruptcy Protection', *Los Angeles Times*, 11 December 1989; Nicolas Kent, 'I Treat All Directors As If They're Dead', *Stills*, May 1985; Janet Maslin, 'The Pollack Touch', *New York Times Magazine*, 15 December 1985; Paul Rosenfield, 'The Inside Man', *Los Angeles Times*, Calendar, 3 December 1989; Peter Wyeth, 'Cutters Way', *Stills*, April–May 1984.

CHAPTER SIX: FIRE-FIGHTERS AND FORTUNE-HUNTERS

Memo from David O. Selznick selected and edited by Rudy Behlmer, published by Samuel French, Hollywood, 1989; *Directing the Film* by Eric Sherman; *The Movie Business Book* edited by Jason E. Squire, published by Columbus Books, London, 1986; *Filmmaking: The Collaborative Art* edited by Donald Chase for The American Film Institute, published by Little, Brown and Co., Boston, 1975; *Working in Hollywood* by Alexander Brouwer and Thomas Lee Wright, published by Crown Publishers Inc., New York, 1990; *Final Cut: Dreams and Disaster in the Making of Heaven's Gate* by Steven Bach, published by Jonathan Cape Ltd, London, 1985; *Warren Beatty and Desert*

Eyes: A Life and A Story by David Thomson, published by Secker & Warburg, London, 1987.

Michael Shulan, 'The Adventures of Baron Munchausen', *Premiere*, April 1989; Nina J. Easton, 'A Mega-Deal for Simpson, Bruckheimer', *Los Angeles Times*, February 1990; Lynn Hirschberg, 'Bernie's Blabfest', *Vanity Fair*, March 1989; Lynda Obst, 'The Ontology of the Pitch', *California Magazine*, October 1985; Carolyn Foster, 'Dialectics of Dining', *California Magazine*, March 1986; Rex McGee, 'Michael Cimino's Way West', *American Film*, October 1980; Ronald Grover, 'You Don't Know Them – But They Know Moviegoers', *Business Week*, 25 May 1987; Elaine Dutka, 'An Interview With Paramount's Top Guns', *Los Angeles Times*, Calendar, 18 March 1990; Tony Schwartz, 'The Emotion of Triumph', *Premiere*, July/August 1987.

CHAPTER SEVEN: PIGGIES IN THE MIDDLE

Adventures in the Screen Trade by William Goldman, published by Warner Books, New York, 1983; *Moguls, Inside the Business of Show Business* by Michael Pye, published by Holt, Rinehart and Winston, New York, 1980; 'The Deal', by David Pirie, an essay in *Anatomy of the Movies* edited by David Pirie, published by Macmillan Publishing Co., 1981; *Hollywood: The Dream Factory* by Hortense Powdermaker, published by Secker & Warburg, London, 1951.

Howard A. Rodman, 'Talent Brokers', *Film Comment*, January/February 1990; *Esquire*, December 1989; Janice Castro, 'Pocketful of Stars', *Time*, 13 February 1989; Michael Cieply, 'Inside the Agency', *Los Angeles Times*, Calendar, 2 July 1989; L. J. David, 'Hollywood's Most Secret Agent', *New York Times Magazine*, 9 July 1989; Kenneth Turan, 'Why Marty Bauer Wears the Black Hat', *GQ*, February 1989; Peter Bart, 'CAA Turns 15 in H'Wood Battle Zone', *Variety*, 7 February 1990; Celia Brady, 'Pillage Talk', *Spy*, February 1990; 'Ixnay on the rape and pillage talk, Zimmer', *Variety*, 22 November 1989; Lisa Gubernick, 'Living off the past', *Forbes*, 12 June 1989; Kevin Sessums, 'The Famous Eddie L', *Vanity Fair*, January 1990; Nina J. Easton, 'How One Letter Has Divided Hollywood', *Los Angeles Times*, Calendar, 30 October 1989; Kim Masters, 'Battle Royal', *Premiere*, January 1990; Celia Brady, 'There's No Business Like Show Business', *Spy*, January 1990; Steve Hanson and Patricia King Hanson, 'The Fortune of Agents', *Stills*, December 1985; David Robb, 'Buchwald, Par experts wrestle in profits bout', *Variety*, 27 June 1990.

BIBLIOGRAPHY

Bach, S., *Final Cut: Dreams and Disaster in the Making of Heaven's Gate*, Faber, 1986; New York: Morrow, 1985.

Ballio, T. ed., *The American Film Industry*, 2nd rev. ed. Madison: University of Wisconsin Press, 1985.

Bart, P., *Fade Out: Inside the Bunker During the Scandalous Final Days of MGM* (title in US, *Fade Out: The Calamitous Final Days of MGM*), New York: Simon & Schuster 1990; Morrow, 1990.

Bordwell, D. et al., *The Classical Hollywood Cinema: Film Style and Mode of Production in 1960*, Routledge, 1985; pbk., 1988; New York: Columbia University Press, 1986.

Brouwer, A. & Wright, T. L., *Working in Hollywood*, New York: Crown, 1990.

Corliss, R., *The Hollywood Screenwriters*, New York: Avon, 1972.

Dardis, T., *Some Time in the Sun: Hollywood Years of Fitzgerald, Faulkner, West, Huxley and Agee*, Deutsch, 1976. op; New York: Penguin, 1981; Limelight, 1989.

Farber, S. & Green, M., *Outrageous Conduct: Out, Ego and the Twilight Zone Case*, New York: Morrow, 1988.

Friedrich, O., *City of Nets: a Portrait of Hollywood in the 1940s*, Headline, 1987; pbk, 1988. New York: Harper & Row, 1987.

Gabler, N., *An Empire of their Own: How the Jews Invented Hollywood*, W. H. Allen, 1989; New York: Crown, 1988; Doubleday, 1989.

Goldman, W., *Adventures in the Screen Trade*, Futura, 1990; New York: Warner Books, 1983; 1989.

Goldman, W., *Hype and Glory*, Macdonald, 1990; New York: Random, 1990.

Gomery, D., *The Hollywood Studio System*, Macmillan, 1986; New York: St Martin's Press, 1986.

Hamilton, I., *Writers in Hollywood, 1915–51*, Heinemann, 1990; New York: Harper & Row, 1990.

Izod, J., *Hollywood and the Box Office*, Macmillan, 1988; New York: Columbia University Press, 1988.

Kanin, G., *Hollywood: Stars and Starlets, Tycoons and Flesh-peddlers, Moviemakers and Moneymakers, Frauds and Geniuses, Hopefuls and Has-beens, Great Lovers and Sex Symbols*, New York: Viking Press, 1974; Limelight, 1984.

Kerr, P., *The Hollywood Film Industry*, Routledge, 1986; New York: Routledge, Chapman & Hall, 1987.

Lehman, E., *Screening Sickness and Other Tales of Tinsel Town*, New York: G. P. Putnam, 1982. op.

Litwak, M., *Reel Power: the Struggle for Influence and Success in the New Hollywood*, Sidgwick & Jackson, 1987. New York; Morrow, 1986.

McMurtry, L., *Film Flam: Essays on Hollywood*, New York: Simon & Schuster, 1987; 1988.

Moldea, D., *Dark Victory: Ronald Reagan, MCA and the Mob*, New York: Penguin, 1987.

Monaco, J., *American Film Now: the People, the Power, the Money, the Movies*, New York: New American Library, 1983; Zoetrope, 1984.

Mordden, E., *The Hollywood Studios: House Style in the Golden Age of Movies*, New York: Knopf, 1988; Simon & Schuster, 1989.

Parish, J. R. et al., *Hollywood on Hollywood*, New Jersey: Scarecrow Press, 1979.

Powdermaker, H., *Hollywood: the Dream Factory; an Anthropologist Looks at the Movie-makers*, Reprint of 1950 ed. New York: Ayer, 1979.

Schatz, T., *The Genius of the System: Hollywood Filmmaking in the Studio Era*, New York: Simon & Schuster, 1989. op; Pantheon, 1989; 1990.

Schatz, T., *Old Hollywood/New Hollywood: Ritual, Art and Industry*, Michigan: UMI Research Press, 1983.

Slide, A. ed., *The American Film Industry: a Historical Dictionary*, Connecticut: Greenwood Press, 1986; New York: Limelight, 1990.

Squire, J. E. ed., *The Movie Business Book*, Columbus, 1986; New York: Simon & Schuster, 1986.

Taylor, J., *Storming the Magic Kingdom: Wall Street, the Raiders and the Battle for Disney*, Viking, 1988. op; New York: Knopf, 1987; Ballantine, 1988.

INDEX

Abdul, Paula 38
Absence of Malice 18, 32, 141, 143
Adventures of Baron Munchausen, The 183–
  5, 197
agents 210–44
Alda, Alan 225
Altman, Robert 162
American Zoetrope 158–9
Apocalypse Now 160
Arbuckle, Fatty 97, 99
Ashby, Hal 151
Ashley, Ted 235
Avildsen, John 225
Aykroyd, Dan 86, 191, 234

Batman 59, 64, 68
Bauer, Martin 212, 222, 225, 231, 237,
  238, 239, 240, 242
Bauer-Benedek (agency) 221, 225
Beatty, Warren 51, 111, 112, 204, 205
Begelman, David 236
Belushi, John 191
Benedek, Peter 28–9, 143, 213, 214, 237
Berg, Jeff 222
Bergman, Ingrid 99
Berman, Pandro S. 153–4, 182
Bernheim, Alain 128, 241
Black, Shane 117, 243
Blaustein, Barry W. 128
Bloch, Bill 221
Bloom, Jake 82
Boorman, John 31, 149, 150, 174
Bridges, Jeff 198
Brillstein, Bernie 191, 220
Brooks, Mel 47–8, 142
Bruckheimer, Jerry 186–7, 189, 190,
  207–9

Buchwald, Art 87, 127, 128, 241

Caan, James 102–4
Cagney, James 100
Carolco Pictures 84, 117, 244
Cash, Tim 230
Caton-Jones, Michael 223
Chandler, Raymond 129, 131
Chaplin, Charlie 97, 98, 99, 152
Chayefsky, Paddy 143
Chervin, Stan 136, 137, 138, 139
Cieply, Michael 35, 38, 222, 223
Cimino, Michael 160, 200
Clark, Jim 175–6
Cohn, Sam 20, 32, 33
Coler, Alexander 19
Columbia Pictures 41–2, 48, 51, 61, 65,
  68, 69, 70, 190, 234, 243
Coppola, Francis 102, 151, 158–60, 161
Cosby, Bill 51
Creative Artists Agency 220–1, 223–4,
  225, 226–32, 234
Crosby, Bing 19
Cruickshank, Jim 144
Cruise, Tom 79, 187, 226
Cukor, George 180

Dafoe, Willem 168
Dante, Joe 157
Davies, Freeman 173
Davis, Bette 95, 100, 216, 218
De Mille, Cecil B. 200, 201
De Niro, Robert 9, 79
De Palma, Brian 156, 225
Dekom, Peter 52, 53, 83, 221, 233
DeVito, Danny 73, 74, 86, 109

Die Hard 82–3
Dietrich, Marlene 100
Diller, Barry 54, 74, 75, 76, 234, 235–6
directors 147–77
Donner, Richard 72
Doran, Lindsay 122, 137, 139
Douglas, Michael 168
Dunne, John Gregory 45
Duval, Robert 79
Dworet, Laurence 243

Eastwood, Clint 151
Eisner, Michael 39
Emerald Forest, The 149–50
Ephron, Nora 120, 121
Epps, Jack 230
Eszterhas, Joe 26, 85, 117, 228, 229, 244
Evans, David Mickey 243
Evans, Robert 186

Fairbanks, Douglas 96, 97, 99, 152
Fatal Attraction 56–7
Faulkner, William 129
Fellini, Federico 178
Field, Sally 141, 143
Fields, Freddie 235, 239
Fisher King, The 198, 199, 203
Fitzgerald, F. Scott 41, 129, 180
Fleming, Victor 180
Fontaine, Joan 99, 100
Foreman, Carl 135
Fuller, Samuel 147

Ganz, Lowell 124
Garrett, Oliver 180
Gere, Richard 89, 91, 95, 225
Gibson, Mel 19, 85, 95, 225
Gilliam, Terry 23, 31, 183–4, 197–8,
    199, 203
Godfather, The 102, 161
Goldman, William 78, 80, 132, 135, 210
Goldwyn, John 116
Goldwyn, Sam 99, 152
Gone With the Wind 180
Gordon, Lawrence 68, 191, 243
Grazer, Brian 194–5
Griffith, D. W. 151–2
Guber, Peter 42, 48, 68–9, 191, 243

Hackford, Taylor 163, 164–5
Hamill, Mark 167
Harris, Tim 33–4, 123, 124
Hausman, Mike 198
Hawks, Howard 78
Hawn, Goldie 92
Hayward, Leland 216–17
Hecht, Ben 129–30, 131, 180
Heckerling, Amy 126
Herman, Lewis 132
Hill, Debra 196–7, 198, 199, 202, 204
Hitchcock, Alfred 155, 180, 181
Hoberman, David 243
Hoffman, Dustin 51, 102, 122, 225, 226,
    230
Hoffman, Peter 84
Holden, William 115, 117
Hollywood
    Press 22–3, 30–1
    status and wealth 19–20
    work ethic 22
Howard, Ron 124, 194, 221
Howard, Sidney 180
Huston, Anjelica 36
Huston, John 40, 143
Huth, Tom 12
hyphenates 141–5

independent film producers 83–4
Ingram, Rex 153
Inter-Talent 221
International Creative Management 221

Janklow, Morton 224
Jones, Dennis 203
Jones, Jennifer 99, 100
Jones, Loretha 31, 186, 200–1, 202, 204,
    206
Josephson, Michael 21–2, 23, 25–6, 30
JVC 68, 191

Kamen, Stanley 225
Kauffman, Victor 48
Kinski, Nastassia 159
Kurtz, Gary 164

Laemmle, Carl 95, 96
Lansing, Sherry 48, 52
Largo Entertainment 68, 191, 243
Last Temptation of Christ, The 161

Lawrence, Florence 95, 96
Lean, David 151
Lee, Spike 94, 204, 206
Lehman, Ernest 135, 136, 143
Leigh, Vivien 99
Levant, Oscar 9
Levine, Thomas 84
Levinson, Barry 221
Limato, Ed 22, 91, 95, 213, 223, 225, 237, 239, 241
Los Angeles 9–11, 13
Lucas, George 127, 144, 148, 156, 157–8, 163, 164, 168
Ludwig, Tony 229
Luedtke, Kurt 12, 18, 32, 34, 141, 142, 165, 166
Lynch, David 221

MacArthur, Charles 130
Mamet, David 25, 115, 143, 149, 151, 161, 162, 164, 198
Mandel, Babaloo 124–5
Mankiewicz, Herman 129
Mankiewicz, Joseph L. 178
Marks, Tony 203
Matsushita Electric Industrial 70
Mayer, Louis B. 40, 41, 99, 152, 178
Mazursky, Paul 141, 151
McElwaine, Guy 42, 102, 228, 229
Medavoy, Mike 235, 243
Mendel, Barry 236
MGM 44, 46, 152
Milius, John 143, 151, 156
Morita, Akio 65, 66–8, 70–1
movie stars 78–114
  box-office appeal 89
  fees 82–3, 84, 85
  sex disparities 91–5
movies
  budgeting 183, 199, 200–1, 203
  idea development 188–9
  marketing 207–8
  opening grosses 79–80
  press promotion 112–14
  video markets 60, 66
Murdoch, Rupert 54, 62, 63
Murphy, Art 42, 59, 76
Murphy, Eddie 79, 87, 88, 127, 128, 242
Murray, Bill 19, 51, 86, 230, 234

Music Corporation of America 70, 155, 216–19

Newman, Paul 141, 143, 172, 173
Nicholson, Jack 19, 38, 87, 91–2, 102, 120, 151

O'Donnell, Pierce 88
Obst, Lynda 190, 191, 192, 193, 194, 196–7, 198, 202
One Flew Over the Cuckoo's Nest 102
Orr, James 144
Outrageous Fortune 93
Ovitz, Michael 26, 39, 51, 223–4, 225, 226, 227, 228, 232

Paramount 46, 56–7, 87–8, 127, 128, 190
Parker, Alan 176
Parker, Dorothy 126, 129
Peters, Jon 68–9, 70, 191, 243
Pfeiffer, Michelle 95
Pickford, Mary 97, 98, 99, 152
Pitt, Louis 105, 109, 231, 235, 237, 242
Pollack, Sydney 95, 122, 141, 147, 148–9, 151, 163, 165, 166, 168–72, 175, 187–8, 221, 227
Pollock, Tom 52, 54–5, 73, 74, 101, 193, 232–3
Powdermaker, Hortense 18, 23, 25, 27–8, 34, 39, 131, 241
Preston, Dean 127
Price, Frank 42, 243
producers 178–209
Puttnam, David 42, 50, 51, 186, 196, 206, 234

Radman, Howard 119
Ramis, Harold 86, 234
Rayfiel, David 165, 166
Reagan, Ronald 218–19
Redford, Robert 151, 171–2, 230
Reeve, Christopher 127
Reiner, Carl 185
Reinhardt, Gottfried 27
Reitman, Ivan 73, 86, 109, 123, 124, 125, 148, 167, 174, 176, 230, 234
Roberts, Julia 91
Robinson, Phil Alden 40, 116, 117, 118, 141
Rodman, Howard 121, 123, 126, 140, 210, 211, 212

Roeg, Nicolas 151
Ross, Steven J. 61–2, 64, 69, 70
Roth, Joe 41, 52, 53–4, 57, 75, 81, 93,
    206, 243
Ruddy, Albert S. 103, 200, 202, 203

Salem, Murray 123
Sarris, Andrew 133–4, 155
Schaffner, Franklin 135
Schenck, Nick 40–1
Schlesinger, John 175, 176
Schrader, Paul 20, 120, 121
Schühly, Thomas 183, 184
Schulberg, Budd 16
Schulman, Tom 122
Schwarzenegger, Arnold 19, 71, 73, 74,
    79, 86, 87, 101–2, 103–11, 112–13,
    123, 125, 242
Scorsese, Martin 31, 156, 161, 172–3,
    177, 221
Scott, Ridley 151
screenplay
    reading 135–8
    rewrites 121–2
screenwriters 115–46
    credits 125–6
    plagiarism 126–8
    teamwork 123–4
Selznick, David O. 99, 130, 155, 178–
    81, 182
Sheen, Martin 160
Sheffield, David 128
Siegal, Herbert 62
Simon, Roger 117, 141, 215, 239
Simpson, Don 186–7, 189, 190, 207–9
Sony 48, 65–70, 191
Spelling, Aaron 19
Spielberg, Steven 20, 156, 157, 174
Stallone, Sylvester 19–20, 72, 79, 84, 86,
    90, 108, 118, 144
Stark, Ray 51
Steel, Dawn 32–3, 42, 48, 49, 56, 71, 85,
    86, 93, 94, 196, 198, 234
Stein, Jules 216, 218, 219
Stevens, George 151
Stewart, James 86, 216, 217
Stone, Oliver 140, 143, 145–6, 151, 167–
    8, 169, 176, 221
Streep, Meryl 79, 91–2, 94, 95, 120
Streisand, Barbra 151, 169

studio executives 40–77
studios
    job insecurity 51, 55
    market research 55–7
    production and marketing costs 71–
    3
    takeovers 61–70
Sturges, Preston 143

Tanen, Ned 24, 48, 51, 52, 55, 56, 57,
    72, 79, 84, 88, 93, 108, 193, 234,
    235
Taylor, Gil 164
Thalberg, Irving 152–3
Thompson, Anne 92
Thomson, David 155
Time Inc 64
Top Gun 75, 187
Total Recall 84, 87, 109, 112–13
Towne, Robert 16, 151, 163
Townsend, Robert 94, 201, 206
Truffaut, François 133, 155, 157
Twentieth Century Fox 41, 42, 45, 46,
    47, 52, 53, 54, 57, 82

United Artists 46, 99
Universal 46, 216

Verhoeven, Paul 109, 113
Vidal, Gore 34–5, 134, 135
Von Stroheim, Erich 152–3

Warner Communications 61–4, 69
Wasserman, Lew 86, 218, 219, 220, 234
Weaver, Sigourney 93–4
Weingrod, Herschel 33, 120, 123, 124,
    136
Wexler, Haskell 151
Wilder, Billy 115
William Morris Agency 221, 223–4
Williams, Robin 198
Willis, Bruce 75, 81, 82
Willow 60
Winger, Debra 230
Wood, Sam 180
Writers Guild 126, 127

Zanuck, Darryl 42, 43, 232
Zanuck, Richard 41, 45, 54, 231
Zemeckis, Robert 157, 221
Zimmer, Jeremy 211, 222, 235, 236,
    237, 238, 240

PICTURE CREDITS

Black and White Photographs